CHINESE IN YOUR POCKET

CHINESE
IN YOUR
POCKET

MORRIS SWADESH

NEW YORK: HENRY HOLT AND COMPANY

To the
CHINESE PEOPLE

whose characteristic friendliness and patience make learning their language a pleasure.

   With special appreciation to my Chinese and American co-workers who helped develop and test out in practical teaching this plan for putting Chinese into your pocket and onto your tongue: Raymond Hsu, Shih-Hui Hua, Shih-Yi Li, J. E. McDonald, Julian Steuer, Lui-Ho Tung, Chuen-Shang Wang, To-An Wang, Chen-Ning Yang.
   And with sincere gratitude to Prof. Yuen Ren Chao for his careful examination of the ms. and his help toward making the English and the Chinese match in spirit as well as in sense.

M. S.

FOREWORD

THERE ARE many pocket-size introductions to Chinese, but few which do so much in so little space as *Chinese in Your Pocket*. Dr. Swadesh's experience in organizing rapid courses for various languages right on the field in Burma and in China has resulted in a book of a live language with live material for use in live situations. But don't take this for one of those handbooks made up in a hurry for men of supposedly low I. Q. to get a smattering of pidgin Chinese. While the style of exposition may be deceptively informal and colloquial, the stuff behind it is basically the same as what you would learn—or ought to—as part of a more formal academic course.

There is no need to enumerate all the special features of the book, which will speak for themselves. But I should like to mention especially the following:

(1) The "learning tips" give the essence of language learning without the paraphernalia of linguistic terminology —which both the author and I love so much.

(2) The system of romanization used here is in general agreement with recent trends. You can't forget to *un*aspirate your *p*'s and *t*'s if they are written as *b*'s and *d*'s to start with.

(3) The over-all characteristic of informality in both the style of description and the language taught not only makes the subject matter interesting, but also brings home the truth that this is the language of real people in their every-day talk.

(4) After you have learned the main structure of the language thru the varied forms of model sentences, the appended Practical Dictionary will enable you to fill in the gaps of your knowledge with practical ideas for saying something new each time.

It is not expected that mastering the contents of this book will give you many hours of college credit or make you talk like a Chinese, in vocabulary, idiom, and style. That must come with prolonged and painstaking study. But seeing that so much of the learning of Chinese has had to consist of the unlearning of wrong things, I am sure that with *Chinese in Your Pocket* in your pocket you will be that much farther ahead.

Yuen Ren Chao

Cambridge, Massachusetts

PLAN OF ATTACK

SUMMARY OF LEARNING TIPS

1. Imitate: Learn to speak understandably by imitating people.

2. Read, speak, listen: When you *see* the Chinese words, *say* them out loud, so you can *hear* them.

3. Use your head: Figure out ways of getting your meaning across.

4. Use Chinese models: Don't translate word for word from English.

5. Use a few memory aids: Find English words that remind you of the Chinese.

6. Speak up: Talk every chance you get.

7. Repeat new words: When you hear a new word, say it out loud.

8. Keep smiling: Be friendly so that people will talk to you.

9. Ask two-way questions: Is it a this or a that?

EXPLANATIONS

A Method for Talking Soon

OF COURSE, *Chinese in Your Pocket* isn't intended to stay in your pocket. It is arranged so you can very soon be sliding its words off your tongue, talking Chinese fairly easily and very understandably. You can be doing this after fifteen to thirty hours spent in learning the following few tricks:

1. You must be able to get the sound of the words from the spelled form (First Session). Later on (especially in the Fifth and Ninth Sessions), you can improve your pronunciation by listening to and imitating the native Chinese with the help of the suggestions and exercises given in this book. Many people have acquired a real native flavor to their Chinese in just this way.

2. You must master about 50 simple basic sentences (Sessions 2, 6, 10, 13), get to know them so well that they are always on the tip of your tongue.

3. You must get the knack of using the basic sentences in practical situations (Practical Exercises), combining them with each other and with gestures, so that they will get all sorts of meanings across.

4. You must learn to take a word out of the Practical Dictionary and fit it into one of the basic sentences in a way that makes good understandable Chinese.

5. You must have fluent knowledge of a few sentences in Chinese for asking people to speak slowly and clearly, and you must know how to ask questions that have to be an-

swered simply with words you can understand. (See especially Tip 9 on Two-Way Questions, p. 30).

The first part of this book is for learning the tricks we have mentioned. The second part is a Practical Dictionary, which gives the simplest Chinese corresponding to common words in English. The aim is to have a dictionary that is small and easy to use; and also to get you to use the common words of Chinese over and over again in different situations, so that you will eventually get to know them and not have to look them up any more.

The language presented in this book is the official national tongue of China, known as the National Language or North Chinese or Mandarin. It is spoken, altho with many small variations, by about 300 million people in Northern, Central, and Western China. Of the other languages in China, some, like Cantonese, are related to Mandarin in the way that Swedish is related to English; and some, like Tibetan and Mongolian, are altogether different. Nevertheless, almost anywhere you go in China, you are likely to find a certain number of people who have learned the National Language, either in school or by travel in different parts of the country. Obviously, this is the best language for the visitor in China to learn. If you plan to settle in a non-Mandarin area, you will want to know the local language in addition.

The variations of Mandarin itself are apt to bother the new-comer in China, just as foreigners are confused by the differences in English as between Boston and Chicago, or as between London and Edinburgh. However, if you talk in the manner explained in this book, you will be quite easily understood by all who speak Mandarin. The chief difficulty comes when you try to understand them. For instance, you have to get used to the fact that much of central and western

China pronounces **san** for **shan** (mountain), and that some areas pronounce **yən** for **rən** (person) or **byən** for **bing** (soldier).

About the Spelling

The spelling of Chinese in this book is based on the official Chinese National Romanization. The advantages of this choice are:

a. It gives an automatic pronunciation of the consonant sounds. That is, if you read the consonant letters with their usual English values, you make either a sound that is exactly right or something that is near enough so that people will have no trouble understanding you.

b. The representation of the vowel sounds is practically identical with that used in familiar spellings of Chinese place-names, such as Shanghai, Shansi, Hunan, etc. This means that anything you may happen to know or find out about the pronunciation of Chinese geographic names will help you learn to read all the other Chinese words in this book.

In a few small points, we depart from the rules of the National Romanization. These modifications are used only to make things still easier for the beginner:

a. The tones are shown by small arrows instead of by changes in the spelling of the syllable.

b. **Dj** is used instead of **j** to avoid confusion with the sound shown with this letter in other systems.

c. **Dz** is used in place of *tz*.

d. An **ə** (inverted *e*) is used for the slightly varying, but essentially single, sound shown by both *e* and *o*.

e. The combination **ir** is used instead of *y* for the special sound occurring after *s* and *sh* and other similar consonants.

f. The spelling **ung** is used in place of *ong*.

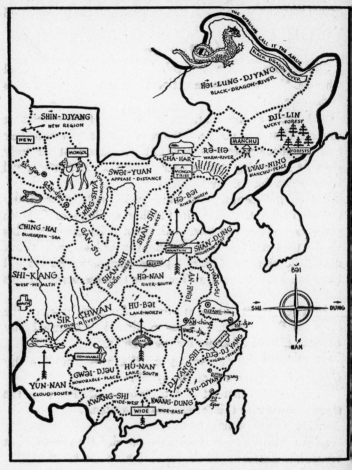

Explanations of these names will be found in the discussion on pages 1 to 7.

ON THE SOUNDS, BEGINNING

FIRST SESSION

PLACE-NAMES AND PRONUNCIATION

Everyone is familiar with a certain number of Chinese place-names: cities, provinces, rivers, etc. You may possibly mispronounce some of them, either because of certain illogical things about the way the consonant letters are used in the conventional spellings, or because of not happening to know how the vowel letters are to be read. Nevertheless, the fact that you are familiar with these names makes it helpful to begin with them in learning to read romanized Chinese.

The Common Spellings

Be prepared for a few striking differences between the National Romanization and the conventional spellings. Here are some cases:

Spellings	*Romanization*	*Meanings*
Kirin	**Dji-lin**	Lucky-forest
Nanking	**Nan-djing**	South-capital
Kiangsi	**Djyang-shi**	River-west
Jehol	**Rə-hə**	Warm-river
Peiping	**Bəi-ping**	North-peace
Tientsin	**Tyan-djin**	Heaven-ferry
Kweichow	**Gwəi-djəu**	Honored-region

1

But a majority of the words appear the same in National Romanization as in the conventional spelling; thus: **Ching-hai** (Bluegreen-sea), **Hu-nan** (Lake-south), **Shan-dung** (Mountain-east).

Meanings as a Memory Help

In this lesson, you will also get considerable information about the meanings of Chinese place-names. This will make it easier for you to learn and remember the names. Furthermore, many of them tell something about where the place is; for example, **Hə-nan** (common spelling *Honan*) and **Hə-bəi** (common spelling *Hopei*) mean respectively *River-south* and *River-north* and are located south and north of the Yellow River. Study the map of the Chinese provinces on page xviii, and you will find you can remember most of the provinces after going over them once.

It is interesting to note that Chinese place-names often refer to desirable qualities and conditions, as **Dji-lin** (Lucky-forest), **Gwəi-djəu** (Honored-region), **Shi-kang** (West-health). The idea of *peace* is most frequent, as in **Bəi-ping** (North-peace), **An-djing** (Peace-felicitation), **Lyau-ning** (Manchu-peace).

Note, incidentally, that there are at least three different roots expressing the idea of *peace* (**ping, ning, an**). And you will find other cases where different roots express approximately the same idea. This is usual in any language. We may also mention that the explanation of some meanings is a little complicated; in such cases, we give the place-names without a translation.

The Arrows

The arrows that you see over the Chinese words, represent the tones—level, sharp-rising, deep-rising, falling—and you must disregard them until you have studied Lesson Five. That they are important is clear from the fact that two provinces, **Shān-shi** (Mountain-west) and **Shǎn-shi** (Shan-region-west, common spelling *Shensi*), would sound exactly alike except for the tone of their first syllables. On the other hand, if anyone tells you that the Chinese cannot understand you unless you get the tones right, that is an exaggerated fairy tale. The fact is that a lot of foreigners mess up the tones and the Chinese can still guess their meaning. So be practical. Since you can't learn everything at once, leave the tones alone for the present.

Vowel Sounds

Pronounce **hu** and **lu** and **wu** like English *who* and *Lou* and *woo*; all Chinese words spelled with **u** at the end rime with these words and with *shoe, do, Lulu,* etc. Pronounce Chinese **yi** and **ni** like English *ye* and *knee*; all words ending in **i** rime with these and with *be, tea, free,* etc. Pronounce **ba** and **sha** like *bah* and *shah*; all words ending in **a** rime with these and with *pa, ah, tra-la-la.* Examples:

hú	lake	**yī**	one	**bā**	eight
lù	road	**shī**	west	**shā**	sand
wǔ	five	**nǐ**	you	**tā**	him
Wú-hú	Wuhu (Weeds-lake)				
Yǎ-lù	Yalu River				
Chá-har	Chahar (named after a Mongol tribe)				

When **n** or **ng** are added to **i** or **u** or **a**, the vowel sound may be changed a little bit. **Lin** and **ling** rime with English *win* and *wing*. The word **dung** does not rime with English *rung* nor with any other English word; however, you can get an idea of the sound if you think of it as being *doong*. Chinese **fang** is not like the English word of the same spelling, but instead is like *fa* of the musical scale with *ng* added. Chinese **fan** has a slightly different vowel so that the word seems almost like our English word, but it is undrawled and still keeps a resemblance to the vowel sound of *fa*. Examples:

lín	woods	lún	wheel	fàn	food
líng	range	dŭng	east	fàng	put

Djí-lin	Kirin (Lucky-woods)
Nán Líng	South Range
Shān-dung	Shantung (Mountain-east)
Kwăng-dung	Kwangtung or Canton (Broad-east)
Ān-ching	Anking (Peace-felicitation)
Nán-djing	Nanking (South-capital)
Hú-nan	Hunan (Lake-south)
Shî-kang	Sikang (West-health)
Djyăng-shi	Kiangsi (Stream-west)
Djyăng-su	Kiangsu (named after two cities, Kiang-ning and Suchow)
Găn-su	Kansu (named after Kanchow and Suchow)
Shĭn-djyang	Sinkiang (New-region)
Níng-shyà	Ningsia (Peaceable-Mongol)

The pronunciation of *an* changes when it follows a *y*: it then may rime with English *tan* or possibly even with *ten*. This changed pronunciation explains why some romanizations use *yen* and *ien* for such syllables. The writing **yan** in National Romanization is based on the principle that this is a modification due to the **y** and not a brand-new sound. Chinese people will understand you whether you remember to modify the sound or let it rime with **shan**. Examples:

Myăn-dyan	Burma
Fú-djyan	Fukien (Named after the cities of Fuchow and Kienyang)
Tyăn-djin	Tientsin (Heaven-ferry)

Combinations with **y** (as in **tyan, myan,** etc.) are to be pronounced all in one syllable, not as in the English name *Lyons* but like the beginning sound of *mew*. Or take the first two syllables of the phrase *to yonder house*, which we can spell **tu yan** or **tə yan**; run it together into **t'yan** or **tyan** and you have the idea of these syllables.

The pronunciation of **u** is different following **y** in the National Romanization. It is then like the French *u* or the German *ü*, a sound with rounded lips as **u** in **lu** but with the tongue lifted toward the front of the mouth as in pronouncing **i** or **y**. However, in the one combination **yung,** there is no difference in pronunciation and such syllables rime with **dung.** Examples:

Modified **u** (except in the combination **yung**)		Unmodified **u** in **yung,** riming with **dung** (*doong*)	
yú	fish	**yùng**	use
nyŭ	female	**shyúng**	bear
chyù	go	**shyŭng-dì**	brothers
yuə̀	month		
yún	clouds		
Yún-nán	Yunnan (Clouds-south)		

The combination **ir** is used for a special sound that has nothing to do with the one in **mi** and **ti.** Our romanized **sir** is a little like the Bostonian pronunciation of *sir*. You can get a reasonably good imitation of the Chinese sound by saying *sir* with the teeth closed together and the point of the tongue held near the roof of the mouth. Note that this sound comes only after **s sh ts ch dz dj.** Examples:

sìr	four	dzìr	written word
shír	ten	djïr	paper
tsìr	stab	**Sìr-chwán**	Szechwan (Four-stream)
chìr	eat		

Pronounce Chinese **hai** and **tai** like English *high* and *tie*; all syllables ending in **ai** rime with these and with *lye, buy, my, eye*. Pronounce Chinese **hau** like English *how*; all syllables ending in **au** rime with *how, plow, now*. Examples:

hăi	sea	**hău**	good
tài-tai	wife	**dău**	island
dài	take along	**yàu**	want
kāi	open	**Lyáu**	Manchu

Shàng-hăi	Shanghai (Upper-sea)
Chĭng-hăi	Tsinghai (Bluegreen-sea)
Hăi-nán Dău	Hainan Tau (Sea-south Island)
Lyáu-ning	Liaoning (Manchu-peace)

There is a somewhat variable sound in Chinese which the romanizations show sometimes with *e*, sometimes with *o*; we have adopted an inverted ə for the reason that it resembles both letters. The sound is made like the *e* in *let* by many Chinese, but most people say it with the sound in *sun, son, rung* or like what dialect writers show by *uh* in *suh* or *thuh*. The syllable ər is like *her* without the *h*; hə is like *her* without the *r*; chəng rimes with English *rung*. Examples:

ər	two	**dzwə̀**	to do
hə́	river	**djə̀-gə**	this one
wə̌	I	**chə́ng**	city
		mə́n	door, gate

hwə̌-chə̄	train (fire-cart)
Chə́ng-dū	Chengtu
Hwáng Hə́	Yellow River
Hə́-nán	Honan (River-south)

When ə comes after **y**, as in **tyə̌** (iron) or **tyə̌-lù** (railroad [iron-road]) or **shyə̀-shyə** (thanks), the pronunciation is like *yes* without the final sound.

Pronounce **bəi** and **həi** like English *bay* and *hay*, and all other syllables ending in əi to rime with these and with *weigh*, *sleigh*, *they*, etc. Pronounce **djəu** like English *Joe* and all words in əu to rime with these and with *go*, *low*, *know*, *toe*, *dough*; the common spelling for this sound is *ow*, as in Fuchow, Hankow, etc. Examples:

bǒi	north	**djəu**	region
gwǒi	honored	**kǒu**	mouth

Bǒi-píng	Peiping (North-peace)
Hə́-bǒi	Hopei (River-north)
Wə́i-hǎi-wə̀i	Weihaiwei (Majestic-sea-guard)
Hə̀i-lung-djyang	Heilungkiang (Black-dragon-stream, Chinese name for the Amur River and the province bordering it)
Gwə̀i-lín	Kweilin (Honored-woods)
Gwə̀i-djəu	Kweichow (Honored-region)
Hwə̀i-djəu	Hweichow (Excellent-region)
Sǔ-djəu	Suchow in Kiangsu province (Cheerful-region)
Sù-djəu	Suchow in Kansu province (Respectful-region)
Fú-djəu	Fuchow
Hǎn-kǒu	Hankow (Han-mouth, that is mouth of the Han River)

LEARNING TIP 1: IMITATE

The way to guarantee that you will be understood when you talk Chinese, is to use the same sounds, tone, and rhythm as the people themselves. And the best way to learn this is by ear and imitation. At your earliest opportunity, get a Chinese to say aloud the words and sentences you are learning, and repeat after him. Thruout this book, you will find suggestions to carry out with 'your Chinese speaker.' This assumes that sooner or later you will be in contact with Chinese-speaking people. Whenever you are, you can carry out any practice you have missed earlier.

There is no harm, however, in speaking less than perfectly at the outset. All learning is by trial and error; that is, you make a stab at the thing, see how you're doing, and then improve on it. If you are generally disposed to listen to the way people talk and to imitate them, and if you take particular note every time they seem to have trouble catching your words, you have a good chance of ending up with a fairly native-sounding accent.

DO THIS: As soon as you have a Chinese speaker to help you, go thru all the examples in this lesson. Let him say each word or expression aloud a couple of times with you repeating after him each time. If two times isn't enough, give it whatever it needs.

You may find that some things are harder than others. The Chinese speaker will let you know if you are getting the idea, and you must try to say things in a way that seems all right to him. However, if there is some little point you fail to get, don't wear yourself and your friend out with it. Skip it for the time being and come back to it later after you have had more opportunity to hear the language spoken.

If you have no one to help you at first, at least make it a point to read the examples out loud two or more times each.

TEST YOURSELF

1. Here are a few miscellaneous items, in English, but spelled in the manner of the Chinese National Romanization. Where an English sound doesn't exist in Chinese, we use the next closest sound. If you read the items out loud,

you should be able to understand them, and you will find this good practice for getting used to the romanization.

(a) Dəu, rəi, mi, fa, səu, la, ti, dəu.

(b) Wən, tu, tri, fər, faiv, siks, səvən, əit, nain, tən.

(c) Sim-pəl Sai-mən mət ə pai-mən,
　　Gəu-ying tu də fər.
　　Səd Sim-pəl Sai-mən tu də pai-mən,
　　Lət mi təist yur wər.
　　Səd də pai-mən tu sim-pəl Sai-mən,
　　Lət mi si yur pə-ni.
　　Səd Sim-pəl Sai-mən tu də pai-mən,
　　In-did Ai hav nat ə-ni.

2. Here is a make-believe map, using geographic words we have run across in this Session. Read the words aloud to test your ability to get the sounds from the spelling. If there is any point you are not clear about, re-read the paragraph that explains it.

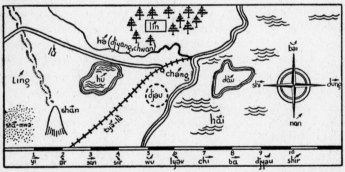

3. Assuming that you have spent several minutes studying the map of the Chinese provinces on page xviii, see how many of the provinces you can now name from memory. Afterwards, check back and note the ones you missed.

EXPRESSIONS FOR GETTING ALONG

SECOND SESSION
SEVENTEEN SENTENCES

Here are seventeen Chinese sentences which will get you just about anything you want, provided you use them cleverly and throw in a few gestures.

English	Chinese	Word-by-word
1. O.K.? *or* Hi!	Hău-bu-hău	Good-not-good
2. Fine, good	Hău	Good
3. Not good	Bù-hău	Not-good
4. Go there	Dău-nă-li chyù	Reach-there go
5. Come here	Dău-djè-li lái	Reach-here come
6. Have a look	Kàn-yi-kan	Look-one-look
7. What's this?	Djè-gə shìr shə́m-mə	This be what
8. What're you doing?	Nǐ dzwè shə́m-mə	You do what
9. Don't do that	Byə́ nă-yang	Don't that-manner
10. Do this	Dzwè djè-yang	Do this-manner
11. I want this one	Wŏ-yàu djè-gə	I-want this-item
12. Give me that one	Gə́i-wŏ nă-gə	Give-me that-item

10

13. How much money?	Dwǒ-shǎu chyán	Much-little-money
14. Where's Peiping?	Běi-píng dzài-shǒm-mə dì-fang	Peiping located-what place
15. You take me —O.K.?	Nǐ dài-wǒ chyù —hǎu-bu-hǎu	You lead-me go —good-not-good
16. Thanks	Shyǒ-shyə	Thank-thank
17. So long	Dzài-djyàn	Again-see

LEARNING TIP 2: READ, SPEAK, LISTEN

When you come to a new Chinese expression, read it out loud. In that way it hits three of your senses: (1) your eye sees it, (2) the muscles of your lips, tongue, etc. have the feel of producing it, and (3) your ear hears it. In this way the impression is fuller and stronger and you have a better chance of remembering the expression when you need to use it. In fact, it is a good idea to say each Chinese word or phrase out loud at least twice whenever you come to it in reading.

Don't be surprised if you sometimes seem to forget expressions almost as fast as you learn them. Chinese is not like French or Spanish or Dutch, where half the words are at least partly similar to the English. As a result you have to use a word twenty to fifty times before it sticks with you. It's easy to keep up your practice if you are in a place where you speak Chinese every day. Otherwise, you have to make up for it by reviewing.

DO THIS: Before you read on, go thru the entire list of sentences two or three times, reading the English and the Chinese out loud.

If you have a Chinese speaker, do it this way: (1) you read the English; (2) the Chinese speaker says the Chinese loud and clear, (3) you repeat after him, (4) the speaker says it again, (5) you repeat a second time. If the book is used in a class or in a study group, the teacher or leader of the group should read the English, followed by the Chinese speaker and then the whole class chiming in.

Explanations

Point 1. The word **hǎu** means *good* or *O.K.* **Bù-hǎu** is *not-good*. Combining both expressions into **hǎu-bu-hǎu** is like saying *Good or not good*, which is the Chinese way of asking *Is it O.K.?* This is about the most useful phrase in the language. You can use it for *Hello* or *Hi* (sentence 1) or as a way of showing you mean to be polite about a request, as in sentence 15, where *You take me—O.K.?* is the same as saying *How about taking me there?* or *Please guide me.*

You can also use **hǎu-bu-hǎu** to ask permission. For instance, the following is like saying *Is it O.K. for me to have a look?*

I'll have a look —O.K.?	**Wǒ kàn-yi-kan —hǎu-bu-hǎu**	I look-one-look— good-not-good

Combine *good* with *look* and you get *good-looking*:

This one's pretty, that one's ugly	**Djè-gə hǎu-kàn, nà-gə bù-hǎu-kàn**	This good-look, that not-good-look

In the phrase **dǐng-hǎu,** which you hear so often, the word **dǐng** means *roof* or *top* or *most*. The general idea is *top-good* or *tops!*

Point 2. To say *is it good?* you say *good-not-good.* The same system is used for other questions. Examples:

Do you want?	**Nǐ yàu-bu-yàu**	You want-not-want
Is it so?	**Shìr-bu-shìr**	Be-not-be
Are you looking?	**Nǐ kàn-bu-kàn**	You look-not-look
Are you coming?	**Nǐ lái-bu-lái**	You come-not-come
Are you going?	**Nǐ chyù-bu-chyù**	You go-not-go
Will you get there?	**Nǐ dàu-bu-dàu**	You reach-not-reach

On the same principle you say *much-little* for *how much?* (**dwō-shǎu**), as in sentence 13. It's like asking *is it much or little?*

However, if there is a word like *what* or *who* or *where* in the sentence, that is to say, a word that is a question in itself, then your question is complete in the simple form. Examples:

What's this?	**Djè shìr shém-mə**	This be what
What do you want?	**Nǐ yàu shém-mə**	You want what
What're you doing?	**Nǐ dzwò shém-mə**	You do what
What're you looking at?	**Nǐ kàn shém-mə**	You look what
Where's Peiping?	**Běi-píng dzài-shém-mə dì-fang**	Peiping located-what-place
Where are you?	**Nǐ dzài-shém-mə-dì-fang**	You located-what-place
Where are you going?	**Nǐ dàu-shém-mə-dì-fang chyu**	You reach-what-place go

Use a question-word with an expression like *want-not-want* and the question-word changes its meaning; for example:

| Do you want anything? | **Nĭ yằu-bu-yằu shᵊ́m-mə** | You want-not-want what |
| Do you do anything? | **Nĭ dzwᵊ̀-bu-dzwᵊ̀ shᵊ́m-mə** | You do-not-do what |

Point 3. There are no words for *yes* and *no* in Chinese. If they ask *do you want* (**yằu-bu-yằu**), you answer either *want* (**yằu**) or *not-want* (**bú-yằu**). If they say *are you doing it?* (**nĭ dzwᵊ̀-bu-dzwᵊ̀**), your answer is either *do* (**dzwᵊ̀**) or *not-do* (**bú-dzwᵊ̀**). It's simple enough, but if you get stuck, you can always get by with one of the following four expressions, which are therefore well worth memorizing:

O. K.	**Hằu**	Good
Not O. K.	**Bù-hằu**	Not-good
It's so	**Shìr**	Be
It isn't so	**Bú-shìr**	Not-be

LEARNING TIP 3: USE YOUR HEAD

Use your head to figure out ways of getting your meaning across with what few words you know. For example, you go to a Chinese mechanic to get your brakes fixed. You say, *Hi, come here, have a look.* When he comes over, work your brake and say, *Not O.K.*

If you follow this system you will not only get what you want but you will also be using the same words over and over till they stick with you. In the end you learn the language a lot faster than the man who is always thumbing thru his dictionary to find the exact translation of his thoughts.

PRACTICAL TEST

What can you do in the practical situations described below? Look for a suitable sentence among the seventeen at the beginning of this Session, or, if you can, do it from memory. Anyhow, say the Chinese out loud with gestures.

1. You go into a silk store to look around. What do you say for *Hello?*

2. The clerk answers your greeting by saying, **Hǎu, shyə̀-shyə. Ní hǎu-bu-hǎu.** What is she saying? How do you answer?

3. How do you ask permission to look around?

4. You see some handkerchiefs and want to know the price for six. What do you say and what do you do?

5. The clerk holds up two $500 bills (Chinese money) to show the price. You don't want to pay that much. How do you tell her so?

6. You want to offer $500. What do you say and do?

7. You settle on $800. Hand her the money and ask if it's right?

8. She answers, **Hǎu. Shyə̀-shyə.** Then she shows you a dressing gown. Tell her you don't care for it.

9. You notice that the clerk is wearing a beautiful scarf. How do you find out if she'll sell?

10. She doesn't want to sell. Instead she goes to the showcase and says, **Dàu-djə̀-li lái kàn-yi-kan.** What does that mean?

11. She shows you another scarf. Can you understand her if she says, **Djə̀-gə hǎu-kàn. Ní yàu-bu-yàu.**

12. You finish shopping. Tell the girl thanks and good-by.

THIRD SESSION

HOW THEY'RE BUILT

If you know how the sentences are put together and what each word means, you will be able to say a lot of new things with the same words. Study the Word-by-word breakdown (third column) of the Seventeen Sentences. Then read the following explanations.

Point 4. In Chinese, as in any other language, there are words that sound exactly like other words. English examples are seen in: 'Don't hide my nail file in the letter file,' 'Blackberries are green when they are red,' 'When the light blue fly came to light on the electric light, I gave it a light blow with a light sledgehammer.' Chinese examples in our Seventeen Sentences are:

> **dzài** meaning both *again* and *located*
> **dzwò** meaning both *sit* and *do, make*
> **shìr** meaning both *be* and *job, work, matter*

As in English, you can tell what is meant by the way the word is used. Can you translate the following:

Wǒ dzài-djè-li dzwò   **Djè-gə bú-shìr Běi-píng**
Wǒ bú-yàu dzài chyù   **Wǒ bú-yàu dzwò shìr**

There are also words that sound alike at first, but are absolutely different once you get used to Chinese tones. This will be discussed later.

Point 5. Notice the following sets of words:

this	djè	that	nà
this one	djè-gə	that one	nà-gə

like this	**djə̀-yang**	like that	**nǎ-yang**
this place	**djə̀-gə dǐ-fang**	that place	**nǎ-gə dǐ-fang**
here	**djə̀-li**	there	**nǎ-li**

The simple word **djə̀** is used mostly when you mean *this stuff* or *this situation* or *this matter*. **Djə̀-gə** is used to refer to a specific person or thing; note that to say *this place* you use **djə̀-gə dǐ-fang**, which is like saying *this-item place*. For *like this* or *in this way* you say **djə̀-yang,** which may be translated *this-manner*. For *it is here*, you can use *located-this-item place* (**dzài-djə̀-gə dǐ-fang**) or *located-here* (**dzài-djə̀-li**). Note that the words for *here* and *there* are made up with the words for *this* and *that* with an added syllable, which means *in*; that is to say, **djə̀-li** for *here* is made up of *this-in* and **nǎ-li** for *there* is made up of *that-in*.

For saying *don't do that* (sentence 9), the most common expression is *don't that-manner*; the word for *do* can be put in but it is not usual. The shorter expression is like saying *not that way* in English.

The Chinese of Peiping use slightly different demonstratives from those listed above: this **djə̀i,** this one **djə̀i-gə,** here **djə̀r;** that **nə̀i,** that one **nə̀i-gə,** there **nǎr.** The greater number of Chinese say **djə̀** etc., but Peiping is the foremost Mandarin-speaking city. So you can take your choice.

Point 6. Chinese sentences are worded much like our telegrams. In general, things that can be easily guessed are left out. A waiter is likely to say *Want-what?* (**yǎu-shəm-mə**) without bringing in the word for *you*, since anyone can see he's talking to you. When you answer, it's enough to say *Want beans* rather than *I want beans*, because he will understand you aren't ordering for your uncle back in Rhode Island. On the other hand, if there are two of you each ordering something different, then you'd say:

I want this,	**Wǒ yàu djǒ-gə,**	I want this,
he wants that	**tā yàu nǎ-gə**	he want that

Point 7. These words are important to know:

me *or* I	**wǒ**	us *or* we	**wǒ-mən**
you (one person)	**nǐ**	you people	**nǐ-mən**
him *or* he	**tā**	them *or* they	**tā-mən**
her *or* she	**tā**		
it	**tā**		

Notice that in Chinese the word for *you* is different according to whether you are talking to one person or to more than one. Otherwise, the words of this set (the pronouns) are simpler in Chinese than in English. Single words go for *me* or *I*, for *us* or *we*, for *them* or *they*. And the word **tā** goes for male or female or object.

Point 8. Study the following expressions, which the Chinese language makes with a clever use of the word for *one*:

Have a look	**Kàn-yi-kan**	Look-one-look
Go for a little while	**Chyù-yi-chyu**	Go-one-go
Sit a while	**Dzwə̀-yi-dzwə**	Sit-one-sit

Point 9. The word for *want* is good to know in any language. Study the following examples, which show different ways of using the word **yàu,** meaning *want* or *will*:

Do you want?	**Nǐ yàu-bu-yàu**	You want-not-want
I want that	**Wǒ yàu nǎ-gə**	I want that
I want to go *or* I'll go	**Wǒ yàu-chyù**	I want-go
I want you to come	**Wǒ yàu nǐ-lái**	I want you-come

Point 10. For telling a person not to do something you can say *not-want*, which is like telling him he doesn't want to do it, or you can use the simplified form **byè**, which we translate *don't*. The short expression is the more usual.

Don't go   **Byè-chyù** *or* **bú-yàu chyù**

LEARNING TIP 4: USE CHINESE MODELS

Never try to make up sentences in English and then translate them word-for-word into Chinese. If you do, you get stuff that sounds as puzzling and odd as the things we sometimes hear foreigners say in English. Instead, make all new sentences on the model of the Chinese sentences you already know. For example, taking the model of sentence 14, *Where's Peiping?* you can make:

Where's Shanghai?	**Shàng-hǎi dzài-shém-mə-dì-fang**	Shanghai located-what-place
Where's the coffee?	**Kā-fēi dzài-shém-mə-dì-fang**	Coffee located-what-place
Where is he?	**Tā dzài-shém-mə-dì-fang**	He located-what-place
The coffee's there	**Kā-fēi dzài-nà-li**	Coffee located-there
He's here	**Tā dzài-djà-li**	He located-here
He's in Peiping	**Tā dzài-Bèi-píng**	He located-Peiping

You see that sentence 14 is made up of two parts, the word *Peiping* and the expression that refers to its location (*located-what-place*). Instead of *Peiping*, you can use the name of any place or person or object. And instead of *located-what-place* you can say *located-there*, *located-here* or located any place you wish. Using this model you can make hundreds of sentences, all of them perfect Chinese.

In the same way you can make plenty of good sentences using the model of sentence 7, *This be what?* For example:

| What is he? | **Tā shìr shém-mə** | He be-what |
| That's Peiping | **Nà shìr Běi-píng** | That be Peiping |

DO THIS: Go over the Seventeen Sentences with your Chinese speaker once more, following the same method as before. Keep trying your best to mimic his tone and rhythm as well as the sounds.

PRACTICAL TEST

Pick out the right answer from the phonies and speak it out loud with gestures.

1. Seeing a friend in a restaurant, you walk up and say:
(A) **Shyè-shyə.** (B) **Shìr-bu-shìr.** (C) **Hǎu-bu-hǎu.**

2. Your friend answers:
(A) **Wó-hǎu, ní hǎu-bu-hǎu.** (B) **Dzài-djyàn.** (C) **Nǐ bu-hǎu-kàn.**

3. She invites you to sit:
(A) **Nǐ lái dzwò, hǎu-bu-hǎu.** (B) **Wǒ bu-yàu nǐ chyù.**
(C) **Dzwò djə̀-yang.**

4. You thank her:
(A) **Dzài-shém-mə dì-fang.** (B) **Shyè-shyə.** (C) **Tā bù-hǎu.**

5. The waiter comes and asks what you'll have:
(A) **Nǐ yàu-bu-yàu lái.** (B) **Nà-gə shìr shém-mə.** (C) **Nǐ yàu shém-mə.**

6. Wishing to order what your friend has, you point and say:
(A) **Gěi-tā nà-gə.** (B) **Yàu nà-gə.** (C) **Yàu kàn-yi-kan.**

7. The waiter asks how you like the food:

(A) Dwə̄-shǎu chyán. (B) Hǎu-bu-hǎu. (C) Dzwə̀-yi-dzwə.

8. It's delicious, so you say:

(A) Dzài-djə̀-li. (B) Djə̀-gə shìr shə́m-mə. (C) Díng-hǎu.

9. You order coffee for the two of you:

(A) Gə́i-wǒ kǎ-fə̀i. (B) Gə́i-wǒ-mən kǎ-fə̀i. (C) Shìr-bu-shìr kǎ-fə̀i.

10. You ask for the bill:

(A) Wǒ-yǎu-chyù. (B) Dwə̄-shǎu chyán. (C) Wǒ bú-yǎu gə́i chyán. (D) Byə̀ djə̀-yang.

11. You and your friend say good-by to the waiter:

(A) Dzài-djyǎn. (B) Nǐ dǎi-wǒ-mən lái. (C) Nǐ-mən dǎu-nǎ-li chyu.

FOURTH SESSION
CLINCHING THEM

By now you are pretty familiar with the expressions in the Seventeen Sentences. It is therefore a good time to try to clinch them in your mind, so you will know them thoroly and be able to use them at any time without stopping to think.

The Cover-Up Method

Cover up the English columns. Read the Chinese aloud and see if you can give the meaning. When you come to one you don't know, look at the English. Having got the meaning, go on to the next expression and the next till you finish. Go thru the entire list again and again until you can do the whole of it without missing.

Then cover up the Chinese and see if you can give it for

each English expression. Always say the Chinese out loud.

DO THIS: Take time out right now, at least fifteen or twenty minutes, to work over the expressions using the memory system just described. After that, go thru all the expressions once more with your Chinese speaker, but this time without looking in the book and without saying the English.

LEARNING TIP 5: MEMORY AIDS

When you're trying to learn words in a new language, it's sometimes helpful to think of some English word whose sound and meaning remind you of the foreign word. For example:

Kids *yowl* for castoria. (**Yǎu** means *want*.)
This is a *jugga* cida. (**Djɜ̀-gə** means *this*.)
Chyu-zit, da cops! (**Chyù** means *go*.)
We *conn* the sea from a *conn*ing tower. (**Kàn** means *look*.)
Gǒi means *give* or *gave* as in *gi*mme and *ga'*eme.
Sure, it is. (**Shìr** means *it is*.)

You can make up silly phrases for any word you especially want to remember. After you've used the word a few times and know it well you can forget the memory aid. You don't want too many trick phrases in your mind because then you can't keep them apart.

LEARNING TIP 6: SPEAK UP

Memorizing words is one thing, speaking a language is another. You must get so that the words **díng-hǎu** or **wǒ yàu nǎ-gə** just naturally come to your mind every time you see something nice. The way to get a direct-fire memory is by using the expressions often in natural situations. Be friendly and talkative. Try to say something every time you meet Chinese people. This will be much easier later on when you learn a few more expressions.

The Practical Dictionary

The short Practical Dictionary at the back of this book contains only the most common ordinary words. It has been kept short not to save space, but so you will use the words again and again until you know them well, instead of scattering your attention over thousands of different words. Look for *help* and not for *assist*, for *big* and not for *colossal*. If you don't find what you want, think of some other way of putting the idea.

PRACTICAL TEST

In this test don't look up more than one word for each problem. Follow Chinese models you know, fitting the new word into the proper place. Your answer is correct if you can be understood by a Chinese.

1. Taking a friend to supper, you ask, *Is this restaurant O.K.?*
2. Order rice.
3. Order beef.
4. Order tea.
5. Ask your friend if she likes the meat.
6. Ask her to pass the salt.
7. Ask her if she'd care to go to the movies.
8. When you see her home, ask for a kiss.
9. She says: **Byó nà-yang.** What does that mean?
10. The rest is up to you. Don't look up too many words,

THE TONES

If you learn to speak Chinese like the people themselves, they will like you for it and they will understand you better. If you have followed instructions about listening to Chinese speakers and imitating them, you must by now have a reasonably good and understandable pronunciation. This Session and the ninth give you drill on points that need special attention.

The tones of Chinese aren't as hard as some people make out. Actually there is no tone in Chinese that we don't also have in English. The difference is that in English we use different tones to show whether we are asking a question or making a statement. In Chinese each syllable has its own tone which stays put regardless of whether you are asking or telling.

1. *Level tone.* Like sounding *Mi-mi-mi*
tā yǐ sān chyǎn shìr (him, one, three, thousand, army division)

2. *Sharp-rising tone.* Like asking in English: *Huh? huh?*
lái chǎ rén chyǎn shír (come, tea, person, money, ten)

3. *Deep-rising tone.* When someone is telling a story, you say *yeah, yeah* to show you want him to go on. Drag it out.
hǎu wǒ nǐ chyǎn shǐr (good, me, you, shallow, dung)

24

4. *Falling tone.* Like an abrupt command; say: *Don't!*
Don't!
dzài kǎn yàu chyǎn shìr (located, look, want, owe, be)

5. *Four tones.* Words that are alike as to sounds and different as to tones, may seem entirely alike at first but not after
you get used to Chinese. It isn't at all hard to distinguish
the sound of **mài** with falling tone, which means *sell*, and
mǎi with deep-rising tone, which means *buy*. The same goes
for the examples given below. First say your English examples, then hum them, then say the Chinese—each twice.

(English examples)

mi	*mi*	*huh?*	*huh?*	*yeah,*	*yeah,*	*don't!*	*don't!*
♩	♪	♫	♫	♪♩	♩♪	♪	♫
hm	*hm*	*hm*	*hm*	*hmm*	*hmm*	*hm*	*hm*

(hum to get the sound)

shìr	**shìr**	**shír**	**shír**	**shǐr**	**shǐr**	**shìr**	**shìr**

(division, ten, dung, be)

chyǎn	**chyǎn**	**chyán**	**chyán**	**chyǎn**	**chyǎn**	**chyàn**	**chyàn**

(thousand, money, shallow, owe)

6. *Weak Syllables.* In some words there is a second syllable
that is very short and weak and whose tone is middle or low
in pitch. Examples:

yā-dz dāu-dz dǔng-shi tā-də (duck, knife, thing, his)
yí-dz lán-dz húng-də wán-lə (soap, basket, red, finished)
yǐ-dz tǎn-dz nǐ-də hǎu-lə (chair, blanket, yours, repaired)
kù-dz dàu-dz djè-gə hwài-lə (pants, mature rice, this,
  spoiled)

Words like **yā-dz** etc. should properly be spelled **yā-dzir;**
that is, they have the vowel sound described on p. 5. How-

ever, in the weak syllable, the effect is like the *dz* of *adze* pronounced with an extra push to the ending.

7. *Simplification of deep-rising.* When a deep-rising syllable is followed by another syllable, as in the examples of the third set in 6, you pronounce a deep tone but don't rise on the same syllable. You hold the deep tone till you get to the second syllable which is on a higher pitch. The two syllables together sound something like our *uh-huh* when used in place of *yeah* to get a person to go on with his story.

Compare the word **yĭ-dz** (chair) with **yí-dz** (soap). The combination of a deep tone followed by a weak syllable on the higher pitch is very different from the sharp-rising tone followed by the middle-pitched weak syllable.

8. *Change of deep-rising.* You may have noticed that deep-rising tones sometimes change to sharp-rising, for instance, *give* is **gŏi** but *give-me* is **gŏi-wŏ**. This happens with deep-rising syllables every time they are followed by another deep-rising syllable in the same phrase, that is, when they are pronounced together without any pause. Examples:

Give-me	**Gŏi-wŏ**	**Gŏi + wŏ**
You-O.K.	**Ní-hău**	**Nĭ + hău**
I-O.K.	**Wŏ-hău**	**Wŏ + hău**

9. *Tone-weakening.* Chinese words, like English, often lose their original accent when they are put into sentences. They may keep a light accent, with the tone less clearly spoken but still recognizable, or they may become weak syllables, like those described under 6.

10. *Rhythm.* The best way to get a good easy pronunciation is to get the rhythm of the whole sentence. Instead of speaking one syllable at a time, learn to speak in natural groups.

DO THIS: Go thru all the examples, with your Chinese speaker. He should say all the examples in a set, not one at a time, so you can get a real impression of the sound. Then you repeat the whole set. If there are several of you, it is a good idea to do the exercises in chorus and then individually. This is so the Chinese speaker can hear your pronunciation and correct you if necessary.

If you have no Chinese speaker, get what you can out of the explanation and skip to the next session.

DICTATION

You will find it helps your feeling for Chinese sounds quite a bit if you try to write down words and phrases you hear. Have your Chinese speaker dictate some words taken from the exercises in mixed order. Write them and then check to see what you've missed. Concentrate on the tones this time.

Try to use the same kind of spelling as we use in this book. That way you'll learn more quickly to read the words in the Practical Dictionary with the right pronunciation.

English and Chinese use the same tones

TALKING UNIT TWO
EVERYDAY CONVERSATION

SIXTH SESSION
CONVERSATIONAL EXPRESSIONS

Trying to talk pidgin English will help give you the feel of how Chinese sentences are built. After this we will give the word-by-word equivalent of the Chinese in the first column. When it's hard to guess the real meaning, we add it in parentheses.

Reach-what-place go (Where are you going?)	Dǎu-shə́m-mə-dǐ-fang chyu
Not-reach-what-place go (Not going anywhere)	Bú-dǎu-shə́m-mə-dǐ-fang chyu
You called what?	Nǐ djyǎu shə́m-mə
I be Lee-Mr. (I am Mr. Lee)	Wǒ shìr Lǐ-Shyan-shəng
You-howabout? (How about you?)	Nǐ-nə
You be what-place-belonging person (Where are you from?)	Nǐ shìr shə́m-mə-dǐ-fang-də rə́n
Be China-person, be America-person (Are you Chinese or American?)	Shìr Djǔng-gwə-rən, shìr Mǒi-gwə-rən
You located-what-place live	Nǐ dzǎi-shə́m-mə-dǐ-fang djù
Have-haven't wife (Are you married or single?)	Yǒu-məi-yǒu tài-tai

28

Have	Yǒu
Haven't	Méi-yǒu
Husband, *also* Mr., gentleman, teacher	Shyān-shəng
Child	Hái-dz
You-belonging father still located-not-located (Is your father still alive?)	Nǐ-də fù-chin hái dzài-bu-dzài
Located (He's living)	Dzài
Not-located-done (He passed away)	Bú-dzài-lə
Mother	Mǔ-chin
You do what job (What's your trade?)	Nǐ dzwò shém-mə shìr
Not-do what job (I have no work)	Bú-dzwò shém-mə shìr
I not-understand	Wǒ bù-dǔng
Again-speak one-time (Repeat)	Dzài-shwō yí-tsìr
You be-not-be soldier	Nǐ shìr-bu-shìr bīng
Work-person-huh? (Are you a worker?)	Gūng-rən-ma
Buy-sell-person	Mǎi-mai-rən

LEARNING TIP 7: REPEAT NEW WORDS

When someone is speaking to you and uses a word you don't understand, repeat it after him once or several times. This gives you time to think; sometimes you remember the word while saying it over. It also gives you pronunciation practice and helps you learn words. Besides, it makes the man realize you are just learning the language, so he may speak more slowly and use simpler words.

LEARNING TIP 8: KEEP SMILING

In making conversation, it doesn't hurt to ask silly questions as a friendly joke. For instance, you can ask a Chinese school-kid if he's American, then if he has a wife, and when he says *No*, ask if he has children.

LEARNING TIP 9: TWO-WAY QUESTIONS

Whenever you hear something you don't understand, you can make a guess as to what it's about and ask, *Is it or isn't it such-and-such*? For instance, if you know a man is trying to tell you his trade, you can say *You be-not-be mechanic*, *You be-not-be driver* and so forth. He will answer **Bú-shìr** (not-be) until you hit the right one and then he'll say **Shìr** (be).

Guessing is always a big help toward understanding. If you know more or less what a man is talking about, it's easier to recognize words you know and to piece together half-understood sentences. It is specially helpful when you're having trouble catching the man's pronunciation. Also don't forget to use gestures and rough pencil sketches as well as words.

PRACTICAL TEST

Ask your Chinese speaker the questions given at the beginning of this Session and see if you can understand his answers. Then let him ask while you answer.

SEVENTH SESSION

HOW THEY'RE BUILT

DO THIS: Spend about 10 minutes practicing the tone exercises of the Fifth Session. Then run thru the conversational sentences in the Sixth Session.

Explanations

Point 11. The word **djyàu** for *called* or *call* can be used of anything, an object or a person or a place or a word.

This called what?	**Djè-gə djyàu shə́m-mə**
You called what?	**Nï djyàu shə́m-mə**
This you-folks call what (What do you call this?)	**Djè-gə nï-mən djyàu shə́m-mə**
Here called what?	**Djè-li djyàu shə́m-mə**
Truck called what?	*Truck* **djyàu shə́m-mə**

In polite conversation, there's a fancier way of asking a person's name. They say *Honorable-name* and you answer *Humble-name Winterbotham*. This phrase is in the Dictionary under *Honorable* but you'd better use the simple expression for now.

Point 12. Chinese for *Mr. Lee* is *Lee-Mr.* (**Lï-Shyan-shəng**), that is, the *Mr.* comes after the name. In the same way, you say *Lee-Mrs.* and *Lee-Miss*. These words are in the Practical Dictionary.

The word **shyăn-shəng** can be broken down to *first-born*. Since there is nothing about man in it, it is not surprising that it is used also for a *teacher* of either sex.

Point 13. Chinese has a few small words that are never

used alone but are always tacked on to other words. The
most important one is **də**, which is like our 's but used in
various ways. We can take *belonging* as a rough translation.
Study the examples:

Here-belonging person 　(Natives of this place)	**Djə̀-li-də rə́n**
Us-belonging job (Our job)	**Wŏ-mən-də shìr**
This be him-belonging 　(This is his)	**Djə̀-gə shir tă-də**
That be soldier-belonging 　(That is a soldier's)	**Nă-gə shìr bĭng-də**
Me-belonging be good- belonging (Mine is a good one)	**Wŏ-də shìr hău-də**
Buy-sell-belonging (Business)	**Măi-măi-də**
He-speak-belonging good 　(His speaking's good, he 　speaks well)	**Tă-shwə̀-də hău**
Do-job-belonging person 　(People who work)	**Dzwə̀-shìr-də rə́n**

Point 14. Tacked-on **ma** is like a question mark that you
speak out loud. We can translate it as *huh?*

You-good-huh?	**Ní-hău-ma**
Me-huh? (Do you mean me?)	**Wŏ-ma**
Located-here-huh? (Is it here?)	**Dzài-djə̀-li-ma**

Hău-ma has about the same meaning as **hău-bu-hău**, so
that **ma** is just another way of asking a question. Expressions like **hău-bu-hău** are considered a clearer way of speaking, but the expression with **ma** is preferred in cases like
Dzài-djə̀-li-ma rather than the long phrase **Dzài-bu-dzài-
djə̀-li**.

Point 15. Tacked-on **nə** can be translated *how about?* but it is used at the end instead of the beginning. Examples:

Him-howabout (How about him?)	**Tă-nə**
Soldier-howabout (How about the soldiers?)	**Bĭng-nə**
Me-belonging-howabout (How about mine?)	**Wŏ-də-nə**

Point 16. Tacked-on **lə** is used in different ways. Often it shows that a thing has happened in the past.

I come-done (I've come)	**Wŏ lái-lə**
We reach-done (We've arrived)	**Wŏ-mən dău-lə**
Him do-done (He's done it)	**Tă dzwŏ-lə**

Sometimes **lə** gives a special meaning which doesn't have to be connected with having done the thing in the past. With some words, **lə** is dropped for the negative and question forms.

Not-located-done (Pass away)	**Bú-dzài-lə**
Correct, not-correct, correct-not-correct	**Dwèi-lə, bú-dwèi, dwèi-bu-dwèi**

Point 17. Since *have* is **yŏu**, you'd expect **bù-yŏu** for *haven't*. But the Mandarin expression happens to be **méi-yŏu** and the phrase with **bu** is generally regarded as baby-talk—like saying *foots* instead of *feet* in English.

Haven't wife	**Méi-yŏu tài-tai**
Have-haven't child	**Yŏu-méi-yŏu hái-dz**
He haven't go (He hasn't gone)	**Tă méi-yŏu chyù**
Go-done haven't go (Has he gone or hasn't he?)	**Chyù-lə méi-yəu chyù**
Go-done haven't (same idea)	**Chyù-lə méi-yŏu**

Notice that you use a tacked-on **lə** to speak of something that has been done but the separate word **méi-yŏu** for what hasn't been.

Point 18. One use of **yŏu** and **méi-yŏu** is to state whether a given object is or is not in a given place. The meaning is about like *there is, there are*.

Here have soldier (There are   **Djə̀-li yŏu bīng**
soldiers here)

Point 19. In Chinese, one word goes both for *soldier* and *soldiers*, one for *person* and *people* and so forth. You judge from the situation which fits. When you need to be specific, you use the word for *one* if it's only one and words like *several, many* or *all* if there are more than one.

Point 20. The word for *still* (**hái**) sounds exactly like the root-syllable of *child* (**hái-dz**). Note the similarity but don't let it confuse you. It's no worse than the English sentence, *He owns a still but is still sober*.

In some parts of China, the word **hái-dz** means *shoe* as well as *child*. In these parts people are confused unless you say *small* with *child* (**shyău-hái-dz**) and specify *leather-shoe* (**pí-hái**) or *cloth-shoe* (**bù-hái**) for *shoes*.

PRACTICAL TEST

Here is a conversation between two men who meet walking along the road. For each question pick out the sensible answer.

1. **Ní hău-bu-hău.**
(A) **Nĭ-də hău.** (B) **Nĭ bu-hău.** (C) **Dĭng-hău, nĭ-nə.**
2. **Dàu-shə́m-mə dì-fang chyù.**
(A) **Dàu-Bĕi-píng.** (B) **Dzài-Bĕi-píng.** (C) **Shr̀ Shàng-hăi-rən.**

3. Nǐ yàu-dzwò shém-mə.

(A) Bu-dàu-shém-mə dǐ-fang chyù. (B) Wǒ-yàu kàn-yi-kan.
(C) Yǒu tài-tai, yǒu hái-dz.

4. Wǒ bu-dǔng, dzài shwò.

(A) Wǒ-yàu kàn-yi-kan. (B) Dzài-djyàn. (C) Dǔng-bu-dǔng.

5. Nǐ shìr shém-mə dǐ-fang-də rén.

(A) Shìr bing. (B) Dzwò-shìr-də rén. (C) Měi-gwə-rén.

6. Nǐ dzài-shém-mə dǐ-fang djù.

(A) Dàu-*Waco*-ma. (B) Byé dzwò nà-gə. (C) Dzài-djè-li.

7. Nǐ-də fù-chin hái dzài-bu-dzài.

(A) Nǐ-də-nə. (B) Dzài. (C) Dwò-shǎu chyán.

8. Nǐ-də mǔ-chin-nə.

(A) Bu-dzài-lə. (B) Shyè-shyə. (C) Tā měi-yǒu hái-dz.

9. Nǐ yǒu-məi-yǒu tài-tai.

(A) Yǒu. (B) Tā-mən yǒu. (C) Gěi-wǒ nà-gə.

10. Hái-dz-nə.

(A) Dài-wǒ-mən chyù. (B) Měi-yǒu chyù. (C) Hái měi-yǒu.

11. Nǐ dzwò shém-mə shìr.

(A) Dzwò-yi-dzwə. (B) Wǒ shìr gǔng-rən. (C) Měi-yǒu
chyán.

12. Dzài-djyàn.

(A) Mǎi-mai-rən. (B) Dzài-djyàn. (C) Bu-yàu.

EIGHTH SESSION

CLINCHING THEM

DO THIS: Spend about 10 minutes on the tone exercises of
the Fifth Session. Then use the cover-up memory method
(see page 21) on the sentences of the Sixth Session.

PRACTICAL TEST

Use the Practical Dictionary but don't look up more than one word for each problem.

1. You see a girl at a dance. You think she is the kid sister of your friend Li in Peiping. Say *Excuse me*.

2. Ask her if she is Miss Li.

3. Ask her if she's from Peiping.

4. Ask how her brother is.

5. She answers, **Tā hǎu**. What does that mean?

6. Tell her you're glad.

7. Introduce her to your friend by saying, *This is my friend, Jack Jones*.

8. Introduce her to Jack's father by saying, *This is Mr. Jones, my friend's father*.

9. Ask Miss Li if she'd care to dance.

10. Ask if she likes the music.

11. Later you go to a tea room. Ask Miss Li what she'll have.

12. Can you say *Good night* without looking up any words?

Expressions built with the word for "Person"

ON THE SOUNDS, FINAL

SHARPENING UP

The main requirement in your pronunciation of Chinese is that you get the right sound in each word, so that people can make out what you are saying. This you have learned from your study of the First Session. However, it is worth your while to review now so as to be sure you have it all straight.

DO THIS: Go thru the First Session again, concentrating on any point you are not sure of. Also review the Fifth Session, on tones.

Beyond speaking understandably, you may want to polish up your pronunciation so it doesn't sound like a heavy foreign accent to the Chinese. This Session discusses and gives practical exercises on sounds that English-speaking people are most likely to pronounce in un-Chinese fashion. However, to make real progress in this, you definitely need the help of a Chinese speaker. If there is none available to you right now, skip this Session.

1. Get your Chinese speaker to pronounce the words:

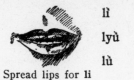

lì   strength

lyù   green

lù   road

Spread lips for **li**

Rounded lips for
lu and **lyu**

Notice that *green* sounds more like *strength* than like *road*. But, if you watch your Chinese speaker as he says the words, you will see that he puckers up his lips for *green* in about the same way as for *road*. In other words, **lyù** is pronounced like **lì** but with the lips rounded; this is the sound that corresponds to **u** in the Romanization every time it follows **y** except in the combination **yung**, which has the normal value for **u**. Here are some words for practice:

> **chì yì nì yǎn**   (gas, idea, you, eye)
> **chyù yù nyǚ yuǎn**   (go, jail, female, far)

2. Ask your Chinese speaker to say:

sìr   four

sə̀   color

Teeth together
in saying **sir**

Mouth slightly open
in saying **sə**

Both words are a little like English *sir*. **Sìr** has the teeth close together and the tongue held high in the mouth; there is something of a buzzing sound to it. **Sə̀** is said with the mouth partly open, the tongue relaxed; like *sub* minus the *b*. Study the sound both by listening and by watching your speaker's mouth. The vowel sound **ir** comes only after *s*- and *sh*- type consonants; we give words with **ə** for comparison:

sìr tsìr dzìr shìr chìr djìr   (four, stab, word-sign, be, eat, paper)

sə̀ tsə̀ dzə́ shə̀ chə̄ djə̀   (color, toilet, duty, shoot, wagon, this)

3. Have your Chinese speaker pronounce these sets of words:

sǎu sǎn tsǎu dzù   (sweep, three, grass, rent)
shǎu shǎn chǎu djù   (few, mountain, fry, live)
shyǎu shyǎn chyǎu djyə̀u   (small, first, shallow, then)

In many parts of central, southern, and western China, the second set of words is pronounced exactly like the first. In the regions that use **sh ch dj**, the Chinese sounds are different from the English, being made with the tongue curled back in the mouth; often it seems as tho they are putting an *r* into the syllable, making our example seem like *srau, sran, tsrau, dzru*. You must try to imitate your Chinese speaker. If you pronounce an ordinary English *sh*, *ch* and *dj*, it may sound to your Chinese friends as tho you were saying words of the third set.

COMPARATIVE TONGUE POSITIONS

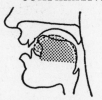
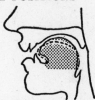

In Pronouncing
Chinese **chau**

In Chinese **chyau**
(same as for **yau**)

English **ch** shown by dotted lines

The third set of words shows combinations with the *y*-sound; the first sounds are modified so they sound in between

English *s*, *ts*, *dz* and English *sh*, *ch*, *dj*. The same modification takes place when *sh* etc. come before *i* (but not the sound which we spell *ir*). Examples:

shi shìn chi chìn-chin dji djìn   (west, new, seven, kiss, chicken, enter)

4. Have your Chinese speaker say:

rðu rén rúng-yi rång   (meat, person, easy, allow)

Some Chinese use a *y*-sound instead of an *r* in these words. The Chinese *r*-sound is made with a rub, so that it slightly resembles the middle sound in *seizure, azure, measure, treasure*, etc. However, it is made with the tongue curled back in the mouth—just like Chinese *sh* etc. as described under 3. If you happen to know Czech, Polish, or Russian, make this sound like the one shown by *ř*, *rz* and *ж* in the alphabets of these languages.

5. Have your speaker pronounce:

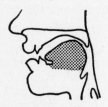

**hǒ hǎu hwà
hěn húng**

(river, good, words,
very, red)

Raised tongue
causing scrape in
Chinese **hau**

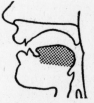

Low tongue sound
without scrape
in English *how*

There is a scrape to the *h*-sound in Chinese, like what is shown by *j* in Spanish, *x* in Russian and Greek, *ch* in Dutch. You can get the sound by mimicking your Chinese speaker.

6. Listen carefully as your speaker says the following:

pàu twěi tsài chū kǎu   (cannon, push, vegetables, out, bake)
bàu dwěi dzài djū gǎu   (report, pile, again, pig, pick-ax)

You may be able to detect the slight difference between each of these sounds and the corresponding English one. Chinese **p t ts ch k** are generally pronounced with much more breath force than the English sounds. Chinese **b d dz dj g** are characterized by having a bit more pressure of the lips or tongue than we have, and the vocal cords do not vibrate. It may occasionally seem as tho you are hearing **p t** etc., but don't let this fool you into changing the sounds. If you get the fine points of Chinese pronunciation, it must not be at the cost of confusing the essentials.

DO THIS: Practice all the examples given under each point above.

DICTATION

Let your Chinese speaker dictate words taken at random from the examples. Write them out and later check your spelling with what is given above.

TALKING UNIT THREE
COUNTING AND ARITHMETIC

TENTH SESSION
FIGURES

One, two, three, four	Yȉ ə̀r sǎn sȉr
Five, six, seven, eight	Wǔ lyə̌u chȉ bā
Nine, ten, eleven, twelve	Djyə̌u shȋr shȋr-yȉ shȋr-ə̀r
Twenty, thirty, forty, fifty	ə̀r-shir sǎn-shr sȉr-shir wǔ-shir
Sixty, seventy, eighty, ninety	Lyə̌u-shir chȉ-shir bā-shir djyə̌u-shir
One-hundred, one-thousand one-tenthousand	Yȉ-bǎi yȉ-chyǎn yí-wǎn
100-tenthousand (1,000,000)	Yȉ-bai-wǎn
One-thousand, nine-hundred, zero, nine (1909)	Yȉ-chyǎn, djyə̌u-bǎi, líng, djyə̌u
Three add-three be-six (3 + 3 = 6)	Sǎn djyā-sǎn shȉr-lyə̌u
Four subtract-one be-three (4 − 1 = 3)	Sȉr djyǎn-yȉ shȉr-sǎn
Correct-not-correct	Dwə̀i-bu-dwə̀i
Correct	Dwə̀i-lə
Not-correct	Bú-dwə̀i
Howmany-item person (How many people?)	Djȉ-gə rə́n

42

Haven't (There aren't any)	**Méi-yŏu**
One-item person (One person)	**Yí-gə rén**
Two-item person (Two people)	**Lyăng-gə rén**
Two-lump-money (Two dollars)	**Lyăng-kwài chyán**
One-item clock (One clock)	**Yí-gə djūng**
One-mark-clock (One o'clock)	**Yì-dyăn-djūng**
One-item clock-head (One hour)	**Yí-gə djūng-tóu**
Five-division-money (Five cents)	**Wŭ-fən-chyán**
Five-division-clock (Five minutes)	**Wŭ-fən-djūng**
Five-mark fifty-division (5:50)	**Wú-dyăn wŭ-shir-fən**
Howmany kilometer	**Dwə̄-shăiu gūng-lĭ**
Five English-mile be eight-kilometer	**Wŭ-Yĭng-lĭ shìr bā-gūng-lĭ**
One-year	**Yì-nyán**
One-ageyear (One year old)	**Yí-swèi**

Explanations

Point 21. The numbers from 11 to 19 are made by combining ten with 1, 2, 3 etc. That is, it is like saying *ten and one, ten and two* and so forth.

Counting from 20 to 90 by tens, you do just the opposite, saying *two-tens, three-tens* and so on. Twenty-one is *two-ten-one*.

Point 22. The Chinese have a special word for *ten-thousand* (**wàn**) and the higher numbers are built up with this word.

Point 23. The word **líng** means *zero*. In giving big numbers you put in the word *zero* in cases like:

1,001 (one-thousand, zero, one) **Yi-chyăn líng yi**
10,050 (one-tenthousand, zero, **Yi-wăn líng wǔ-shir**
fifty)

If you hear someone say **yì-băi-ər**, that is short for **yì-băi-ər-shir,** meaning 120 and not 102. In the same way **yì-chyăn-wǔ** (one-thousand-five) is short for 1,500.

COUNTING

Do each exercise over and over till it comes easily.

1. Count from one to 10 and backwards from 10 to one.
2. To 20 and back by twos.
3. To 30 and back by threes.
4. To 40 and back by fours.
5. To 50 and back by fives.
6. To 100 and back by tens.
7. To 110 and back by elevens.
8. To 120 and back by twelves.
9. To 1000 by hundreds.
10. To 10,000 by thousands.
11. To 100,000 by tenthousands.
12. Read the following numbers out loud:

18	119	2002	30,003	12,345
41	190	2020	33,300	54,321
72	109	2200	30,300	93,713

ELEVENTH SESSION
HOW THEY'RE BUILT

DO THIS: Spend about 10 minutes practicing the sounds in the Ninth Session. Then go thru the expressions given in the Tenth.

Explanations

Point 24. The expression for *nothing* is different from the word for *zero.* You say *It isn't what* (**Bú-shìr shém-mə**) for *It's nothing. There aren't any* is **méi-yǒu** (haven't).

Point 25. When you count things in Chinese, you have to throw in a word, called a classifier, which describes the thing in a general way, something like what we do in English when we say, *one head of cattle, one stick of wood, one round of ammunition.* In Chinese, it goes much farther and you say, for example: one-stem pencil, one-sheet map, one-structure house, one-strip road, and so forth. You can find the more important classifiers in the Practical Dictionary under the word *one,* but better not bother about them. For now, you can get along very well by always using the syllable **gə,** the same as in **djə̀-gə** (this) and **nà-gə** (that). This is the right classifier for words referring to people, most animals and all objects not otherwise classified. Furthermore, the Chinese themselves often use it in place of other syllables.

Try to get into the habit of using **gə** whenever you speak of a given number of anything, for example:

Here have howmany-item person (How many people are there here?)	**Djə̀-li yǒu djǐ-gə rén**
Have three-item (There are three)	**Yǒu sān-gə**

Point 26. The numbers can also be combined with measure-words, that is, words that give units of amount, like: one-package, one-pair, one-lump, one-liter, one-kilometer, one-day, one-year and so forth. A few of the measure words are given in the Tenth Session. Find the others in the Practical Dictionary when you need them.

Note that one-lump (**yí-kwài**) is used for loaves of bread, cakes of soap, dollars of money etc.

Also note that a year of age is expressed differently from a year's length of time.

How many years?—Five years   **Djǐ-nyán—Wǔ-nyán**
How old?—Five years old   **Djǐ-swài—Wǔ-swài**

Point 27. For weights and measures, the Chinese use many different systems. The easiest of them is the metric system, the same as that used in many other parts of the world. In case you don't know: 100 centimeters = 1 meter, 1000 meters = 1 kilometer; 1000 grams = 1 kilogram, 1000 kilograms = 1 metric ton, which is 2200 pounds. A liter is a little more than an American quart. For length, 5 centimeters = 2 inches, 9 meters = 10 yards, 8 kilometers = 5 mi.

You will find the metric units in the Practical Dictionary. All of them begin with the word **gǔng** meaning *public* or *universal.* When the Chinese speak of our units they use **Yîng** for *English.*

Point 28. **Fēn**, meaning *division*, is used for various small units of measure. In the metric system, **gǔng-fēn** is either a gram or a centimeter. And **fēn** is also used for money and time:

Five-division-money (five cents)   **wǔ-fēn-chyán**
Five-division-clock (five minutes)   **wǔ-fēn-djǔng**

Point 29. Numbers used with **djǔng,** meaning *bell* or *clock,* can express the number of clocks or of hours or the time of day:

one-item clock (one clock)   **yí-gə djǔng**
one-item clock-head (one hour)   **yí-gə djǔng-tɕóu**
one-mark-clock (one o'clock)   **yì-dyǎn-djǔng**

To give time in hours and minutes, the expression can be shortened:

five-mark fifty-five (5:55)   **wú-dyǎn wǔ-shir-wǔ**

Point 30. There are two words for *two*: **ər** is used in saying the number by itself and in making higher numbers. **Lyǎng** is used with classifiers and measure-words, when speaking of just two, but not for 22 or 200 and so forth.

one, two, three, four	**yì ər sān sìr**
two-hundred-twenty-two	**ər-bǎi-ər-shir-ər**
two people	**lyǎng-gə rə́n**
twenty-two people	**ər-shir-ər-gə rə́n**
two o'clock	**lyǎng-dyǎn-djüng**
twelve o'clock	**shír-ər-dyǎn-djüng**

However, getting the two words mixed up will not prevent people from understanding you.

Point 31. The word **djǐ** means either *a few, several* or *how many*? In speaking of large numbers, **dwə̄-shǎu** (much-little) is used. For example, **dwə̄-shǎu** is usual in talking about money, **djǐ** in speaking of a person's age:

How much money?	**Dwə̄-shǎu-chyǎn**
How old are you?	**Ní djǐ-swə̀i**

PRACTICAL TEST

1. Count out loud the people in each of these groups, saying: **yí-gə rə́n, lyǎng-gə rən, sān-gə rən,** etc.

(A)   (B)   (C)

2. (A) Count everybody in problem one. (B) Count all the men. (C) All the women.

3. Count the clocks in each group, saying; **yí-gə djüng, lyǎng-gə djüng,** etc.

(A)   (B)

(C)

4. (A) Count all clocks in problem three. (B) All alarm clocks. (C) All mantel clocks.

5. Tell the time on each clock:

6. Answer the following questions about yourself: (A) **Ní djǐ-swèi.** (B) **Yǒu djǐ-gə hái-dz.** (C) **Nǐ-də fù-chin djǐ-swèi.** (D) **Nǐ-də mǔ-chin djǐ-swèi.**

7. (A) Name the present year. (B) What was it twelve years ago? (C) 140 years ago? (D) What will it be 100 years from now?

8. Read out loud and give in Chinese the solutions to the following problems:

(A) **Yí-gə djüng shìr wǔ-kwài-chyán. Wǔ-gə djüng shìr dwē-shǎu chyán.**

(B) **Yí-gə güng-rən yǎu chi-kwài-chyán. Sān-gə rən yǎu dwē-shǎu chyán.**

(C) **Wǒ-yǒu sìr-kwài-chyán, ní yǒu sān-kwài, tā yǒu shír-kwài. Wǒ-mən yǒu dwē-shǎu chyán.**

TWELFTH SESSION
CLINCHING THEM

DO THIS: Spend about 10 minutes on the tone exercises of the Fifth Session. When you count or do simple arithmetic problems, try not to get into a sing-song and forget about the proper tones of the words. Keep your tones correct all the time.

Use the cover-up method on the expressions of the Tenth Session.

PRACTICAL TEST

1. Read off the following addition problems, giving the answer along with the problem, like this:

> Problem: 3　+　3　=
> You say: **săn djyă-săn shìr-lyău**

(A) 1+0=	(B) 1+1=	(C) 1+2=	(D) 1+3=
(E) 1+4=	(F) 1+5=	(G) 1+6=	(H) 1+7=
(I) 1+8=	(J) 1+9=	(K) 2+2=	(L) 4+4=
(M) 5+5=	(N) 2+5=	(O) 3+4=	(P) 5+2=
(Q) 4+5=	(R) 3+3=		

2. Read off these subtraction problems:

> Example: 3　—　3　=
> You say: **săn djyăn-săn shìr-líng.**

(A) 10−2=	(B) 10−3=	(C) 10−4=	(D) 10−5=
(E) 10−6=	(F) 9−7=	(G) 4−3=	(H) 2−1=
(I) 7−3=	(J) 9−3=	(K) 9−4=	(L) 6−2=

3. Using the Practical Dictionary when necessary, ask and answer the following questions:

(A) How many brothers have you?
(B) How many sisters have you?
(C) How many friends have you in St. Louis?
(D) How many people are there here?
(E) One cup of coffee is fifty dollars. How much is ten cups?

THIRTEENTH SESSION
TALKING BUSINESS

You know-not-know (Do you know?)	**Nǐ djǐr-dàu bu-djǐr-dàu**
Wang-Mr. located-what-place (Where's Mr. Wang?)	**Wáng-Shyan-shəng dzài shə́m-mə dì-fang**
He reach-store-in go-done (He's gone to the store)	**Tā dàu-pù-dz-li chyù-lə**
Buy things (to buy things)	**mǎi dūng-shi**
Eh? or Huh? (What did you say?)	**Á**
Face-not-up (I'm in the wrong, I'm sorry)	**Dwèi-bu-chǐ**
Invite again-speak one-time (Please repeat)	**Chǐng dzài-shwō yí-tsìr**
I not-be China-person	**Wǒ bú-shìr Djūng-gwə-rən**
I not-understand	**Wǒ bù-dǔng**
Not-knowhow speak China-words	**Bú-hwèi shwō Djūng-gwə-hwà**
I-understand-belonging very little (My understanding is very little)	**Wǒ-dǔng-də hə́n-shǎu**
Don't speak-belonging too-fast (Don't speak too fast)	**Byə̀ shwō-də tài-kwài**

51

Wang-Mr. what-time return-come (When'll Mr. Wang come back?)	**Wáng-Shyan-shəng shə́m-mə shír-həu hwə́i-lai**
Howmany-mark clock (What o'clock?)	**Djǐ-dyǎn-djǔng**
Return-come-belonging time (When he comes back)	**Hwə́i-lai-də shír-həu**
Invite-tell-him (please ask him)	**Chǐng-djyǎu-ta**
Give-me take-this-pants patch-one-patch (to mend these pants for me)	**gə́i-wə̌ bǎ-djə̀-gə-kù-dz bǔ-yi-bu**
Pickup-him go (Take them)	**Ná-ta chyu**
Put located-there (Put them there)	**Fàng dzài-nǎ-li**
Much-thanks	**Dwə̄-shyə̀**

Explanations

Point 32. Many words, of the kind called nouns, end in **dz** when they stand alone, but drop this ending when they are used in combinations with other words. Examples:

store, book-store	**pù-dz, shü-pù**
knife, stab-knife (bayonet)	**dāu-dz, tsȉr-dāu**

On the same principle, a great many two-syllable words in Chinese are simplified to one syllable when used in combinations. Examples:

machine, fly-machine (airplane)	**dji-chȉ, fə̄i-dji**
peace, North-peace (city of Peiping)	**hə́-píng, Bə̌i-ping**
thanks, many thanks	**shyə̀-shyə, dwə̄-shyə̀**

Point 33. The word **hǝn** can sometimes be translated as *very*, but in other cases it seems to be used to round an expression out into two syllables. In these cases, it is better to think of **hǝn** as meaning *rather*.

He speak-belonging rather-fast (He speaks fast)	**Tā-shwǝ̄-dǝ hǝ́n-kwài**
We person rather-much (We are many people. There are a lot of us)	**Wǝ̌-mǝn rǝ́n hǝ̌n-dwǝ̄**

Point 34. Notice the way you put your words together to say *he talks fast*. Follow the same model in saying things like:

He-do-belonging good (He does well)	**Tā-dzwò-dǝ hǎu**
I Chinese-language speak-belonging not-good (I don't speak Chinese well)	**Wǝ̌ Djūng-wǝ́n shwǝ̄-dǝ bu-hǎu**

Point 35. Our word *know* translates several different Chinese words. These include **hwòi** for knowing how to do a thing and **djir-dàu** for knowing a fact or an object.

Me knowhow-do (I know how to do it)	**Wǝ̌ hwòi-dzwò**
Me not-know that word	**Wǝ̌ bù-djir-dàu nà-gǝ hwà**

In the Practical Dictionary you will find still another word for *know, be acquainted with a person*. Whenever you look up a word, you must notice the different Chinese equivalents and decide from the explanations and examples which one fits your meaning.

Point 36. Our advice to you has been never to translate word-for-word from English. This is particularly true of

words like *to*. If you look in the Dictionary, you will find
three different equivalents. In cases like *he wants to go, he
came to see me, it is good to eat*, you simply forget about it.
For going to, you use **dầu** meaning *reach*. For sending or
selling or handing a thing to a person, you use the word for
give. Example:

He reach-Peiping come sell- thing give-me (He comes to Peiping to sell things to me)	**Tä dầu-Bǒi-píng lái mǎi-** **dǔng-shi gǒi-wǒ**

Point 37. **Gǒi**, meaning *give*, is also the most usual equivalent of *for* when you speak of doing something for someone.
In this use, the **gǒi** comes ahead of the main verb.

He give-me do-job (He works for me)	**Tä gǒi-wǒ dzwǒ-shìr**

Point 38. In the First Session you learned to use *Is it
O.K.?* in asking a favor; now you get the regular word for
please, which is the same as *invite*.

Invite-come (Please come)	**Chǐng-lái**
Invite-you come (same meaning)	**Chíng-nǐ lái**
I-invite-him come (I invite him to come)	**Wǒ-chǐng-tä lái**

Point 39. The ideas of bringing and taking in Chinese are
broken into two parts, handling the thing and going or
coming.

Lead-me go (Take me along)	**Dǎi-wǒ chyu**
Lead-him come (Bring him along)	**Dǎi-ta lái**

Pickup-come (Bring it)   **Ná-lai**
Pickup-clock go (Take the   **Ná-djŭng chyu**
   clock)

Similarly, various kinds of action on specifically indicated objects are expressed with the help of the word **bǎ**, which means *take hold*, as in these examples:

Take-that patch-one-patch   **Bǎ-nà-gə bǔ-yi-bu**
   (Mend that)
Take-this look-one-look   **Bǎ-djè-gə kàn-yi-kan**
   (Look this over)
Take-clock buy (Buy the   **Bǎ-djŭng mǎi**
   clock)

Point 40. The word for telling a person to do something is **djyàu** and sounds exactly like the word for *call* or *called*.

This called pants   **Djè-gə djyàu kù-dz**
Tell-him come   **Djyàu-ta lái**

Point 41. **Hwéi,** meaning *return*, sounds like **hwèi,** meaning *know how*, except for the tone. Here's a sentence to practice on:

I not-knowhow return-go   **Wǒ bú-hwèi hwéi-chyu**
   (I don't know how to go
   back)

PRACTICAL TEST

Solve by looking for any words you need among the expressions at the beginning of this Session.

1. You meet a friend. Ask where he's going.
2. He says: **Dàu-pù-dz-li.** What does this mean?
3. Ask him what he intends to buy.

4. He answers: **Hě̃n-dwǒ düng-shi.** What does this mean?

5. Supposing you don't understand, how do you say so?

6. If your friend talks too fast, what do you say?

7. How do you ask him to repeat?

8. Ask your friend if it is a good store.

9. Ask him if they have clocks.

10. Ask him to please buy a clock for you.

11. He says: **Wǒ gěi dwǒ-shǎu chyán.** What does that mean? Give him an answer.

12. Your friend asks what time it is. Tell him you don't know.

13. Say: *When you buy the clock, I'll know what time it is.*

14. Your friend says: **Hě̃n-hǎu. Dzài-djyàn.** What is the meaning? Tell him: *Many thanks.*

FOURTEENTH SESSION
GENERAL REVIEW

DO THIS: Run thru the sentences in the Thirteenth Session with your Chinese speaker. Then use the cover-up method on them.

To Help You Understand

Some expressions given in the Thirteenth Session can be helpful when you are trying to understand people speaking. You can say: *Eh? I'm sorry, Please repeat, I don't understand, I understand very little, Don't speak too fast.* Learn these phrases by heart.

PRACTICAL TEST

Pick out the right replies.

1. **Nǐ dzwǒ shě̃m-mə shìr.**

(A) **Dzwə̀ kù-dz.** (B) **Dzwə̀ dzài-pù-dz-li.** (C) **Gə̌i-tài-tai chyán.**

2. **Nǐ hwə̀i-bu-hwə̀i bǔ wə̌-də kù-dz.**

(A) **Hwə̀i-shwə̄ Djǔng-gwə-hwà.** (B) **Bu-djïr-dǎu.** (C) **Djə̀-gə djyàu shə́m-mə.**

3. **Chǐng kàn-yi-kan.**

(A) **Hǎu.** (B) **Dǎu-pù-dz-li chyu.** (C) **Wə̌ shìr Lǐ-Tai-tai.**

4. **Ní yə̌u-məi-yə̌u shír-həu bǔ djə̀-gə.**

(A) **Wǔ-gə rén.** (B) **Dwə̄-shǎu-dǔng-shi.** (C) **Yə̌u.**

5. **Wə́ djǐ-dyǎn-djǔng hwə́i-lai.**

(A) **Wú-dyǎn-djǔng.** (B) **Wə̌ bu-dzwə̀ shə́m-mə.** (C) **Mə́i-yə̌u djǔng.**

6. **Dwə̄-shǎu chyán.**

(A) **Hə̌n-dwə̄ bing.** (B) **Dwə̄-shyə̀.** (C) **Yí-kwài Mə̌i-gwə-chyán.**

7. **Chǐng dzài-shwə̄ yí-tsìr.**

(A) **Mə́i-yə̌u shír-həu.** (B) **Mǎi-mai-rən.** (C) **Yí-kwài Mə̌i-gwə-chyán.**

REVIEW TEST

Give the Chinese for the following words. Perfect score 120. If you miss more than 30, better do some reviewing.

1. China, America, person, child, wife, husband, mother, father, teacher, workman.

2. Mr., Mrs., merchant, soldier, I, you, he, she, it, we.

3. They, them, you-folks, him, her, here, there, where, what, when.

4. Still, again, how much, what o'clock, how many years, how old, five dollars, five minutes, five cents, five kilometers.

5. Zero, 1, 2, 3, 4, 5, 6, 7, 8, 9.

6. 10, 20, 30, 40, 50, 60, 70, 80, 90, 100.

7. 1000, 10,000, add, subtract, money, store, pants, clock, thing, time.

8. Buy, sell, come, go, do, make, work, sit, look, want.

9. Give, take, bring, understand, know, know how, tell to do, repair, return, invite.

10. Bring, take, take along, pick up, put, located, reach, good, bad, fast.

11. Much, little, correct, fairly, very, too, is, am, are, be.

12. His, yours, he's come, how about that? excuse me, it's so, it isn't so, hello, good-by, thanks.

FIFTEENTH SESSION

CHOOSE YOUR OWN SUBJECT

In using the Practical Dictionary, remember it has only some of the most common words. If you don't find a word, think of another way of saying the same thing or of describing it.

If you expect to talk a lot about certain special things that aren't to be found in this Dictionary, make a list of the words on the blank pages at the end. Be practical rather than ambitious in making your list. Remember that long lists are hard to use. You can get the words for your special list from an interpreter or a large dictionary or by pointing at things and asking Chinese people: **Djə̀-gə djyàu shə́m-mə.**

Unless you are in an awful hurry, when you look up a word in the Practical Dictionary, take a moment to study the various details that are given about the word: other English meanings of the same word, the meaning of the parts of compound forms, examples showing how to use the expression, other Chinese words that sound alike and may cause confusion. This additional information helps you to use the word correctly and to remember it more easily.

Suggestions for the Typewriter: If you expect to be typing out things in Romanized Chinese, you can use plain *e* instead of ə. If you want to include tone-signs, you can have a set of accent marks (ˉ ˊ ˇ ˋ) installed on your machine, to be used in place of the arrows. A French typewriter has ˊ and ˋ and these can be combined into ˇ; for the level tone a hyphen can be used by turning the roller slightly to space it higher.

PRACTICAL TEST

Using the Practical Dictionary, carry on a conversation on any topic, such as those suggested below. You can do it as make-believe with your Chinese speaker or, better yet, in a real situation. It is a good idea to prepare for this test by thinking in advance of some of the things you'll want to say and making a list of words you will need.

1. An invitation to a Chinese home. Conversation about family and friends, interests, work, food.

2. Take something to a shop to be repaired or cleaned. Explain what is to be done, ask the cost and when it will be ready.

3. A little shopping trip.

4. Interview a man you want to hire. Ask what he can do, where he worked before, etc. Arrange about salary and explain duties.

5. Demonstrate and explain how to start and drive a car, or how to handle some other piece of machinery.

6. Ask information from a local farmer about how to get to a given place, condition of the road, etc.

HAU-BU-HAU

Knowing the Chinese words **hau** (good) and **bu-hau** (not-good) is a big help. This little story can be understood after learning the Seventeen Sentences of the Second Session.

A PRACTICAL CHINESE DICTIONARY

A

a **yí-gə** (*same as* one, *but commonly omitted*; *also see other forms listed under* one)

ability, skill **gūng-fu** (*also* spare time)

able to **néng**: I'm able to do it **wǒ néng-dzwò** (I able-do)

about, concerning **dǎu** (*same as* reach): they talk about him **tā-mən shwǒ-dǎu-ta** (they speak-reach-him), think about that **shyǎng dǎu-nà-gə** (think reach-that)

about, more or less **chà-bu-dwǒ** (difference-not-much): about thirty **chà-bu-dwǒ sān-shir-gə**

above, on **shàng** (*same as* up) *or* **shàng-byan** (up-side): above the mountain **dzài-shān shàng-byan** (located-mountain up-side)

accelerator, throttle **chì-mǎn** (gas-door)

account **djàng**

accountant **gwǎn-djàng-də** (manage-account-belonging)

acid **swān** (*also* sour): hydrochloric acid **yán-swān** (salt-acid), sulfuric acid **lyóu-swān** (sulfur-acid)

across **héng** (*same as* crosswise) *or* **gwò** (*same as* to cross): there's a stick across the road **yǒu gùn-dz héng dzài-lù-shang** (have stick across located-road-on), he goes across the road **tā dzǒu gwò-lù chyu** (he walk across-road go)

act, perform **yǎn-shí** (perform-drama)

act, pretend to be **djyǎ-djwāng**

actor **shì-dz** *or* **yǎn-yuán** (perform-personnel)

add up **djyā-chi-lai** (add-up-come): add it up **bǎ-ta djyā-chi-lai** (take-it add-up-come)

6 1

adjust **tyáu-djǒng**

adult **dà-rən** (big-person)

advance **chyán-djìn** (front-enter)

advertise **dēng-gwǎng-gàu** (mount-broad-inform)

advertisement **gwǎng-gàu**

advice, suggestion **djú-yi**

advise **chū-djú-yi** (out-suggestion)

afraid, afraid of **pà**: I'm afraid of it **wǒ pà-ta** (I afraid-it)

after **yǐ-hǒu**: he left after I came **wǒ-lái-lə yǐ-hǒu tā djyǒu dzǒu-lə** (I-come-done after, he then leave-done)

afternoon **shyà-wǔ** (down-noon): I'll go in the afternoon **wǒ shyà-wǔ chyù** (I afternoon go)

afterwards **hǒu-lái** (behind-come)

again **yǒu** (*referring to the past*) *or* **dzài** (*referring to future*): he came again **tā yǒu lái-lə** (he again come-done), say it again **dzài-shwǒ** (again-speak)

again and again **yí-tsìr yǒu yi-tsir** (once again once)

against, not in favor **bú-dzàn-chéng** (not-agree)

age **swèi** (*meaning* years old): what's his age **tā djǐ-swèi** (he howmany-years), thirty years of age **sān-shir-swèi** (three-ten-years)

agent, representative **dài-byǎu** (substitute-represent)

agency, branch office **fēn-háng** (division-firm)

ago **yǐ-chyán** (*same as* before): one month ago **yí-gə yuè yǐ-chyán** (one-item month before)

agree **túng-yǐ** (same-mind): I agree with you **wǒ gēn-nǐ túng-yǐ** (I with-you same-mind)

ahead, first **shyān**: go on ahead **nǐ shyān-dzǒu** (you first-walk)

aim, take aim **myáu-djǔn** (sight-accurate)

air **kūng-chì** (air-gas): air force **kūng-djyǔn** (air-army), air raid **kūng-shí**

airfield **fēi-dji-chǎng** (airplane-field)

airplane **fēi-djî** (fly-machine)

alarm **djĭng-bàu** (warning-report)

alcohol **djyŏu-djĭng** (wine-essence)

alive, living **hwŏ-dj** (live-remain): he's still alive **tā hái hwŏ-dj** *or* **tā hái-dzài** (he still-located)

all **dōu** (*also* both): all of you come **nĭ-mən dōu-lái** (youfolks all-come)

all clear! **djyŏ-chú** (loosen-remove)

allied country **túng-méng-gwó** (same-oath-country)

allow, let **djŭn**: let him go **djŭn-ta chyù**

allowed, permissible **kŏ-yi**: smoking isn't allowed here **djŏ-li bù-kŏ-yi chōu-yān** (here not-allowed suck-tobacco), I'm not allowed to go **wŏ bù-kŏ-yi chyù** (I now-allowed go)

almost, more or less **chà-bu-dwō** (difference-not-much)

alone **yí-gə-rən** (one-person): I live alone **wŏ yí-gə-rən djù** (I one-person live)

along, alongside **shùn-dj**: along the river **shùn-dj hó**

aloud **dà-shōng** (big-sound): he spoke aloud **tā dà-shōng shwō-hwà** (he big-sound speak-word)

alphabet **dzìr-mŭ** (word-mother)

already **yĭ-djĭng** (finish-pass): he has already come **tā yĭ-djĭng lái-lə** (he already come-done)

also **yŏ** (*sounds like* wild): he also comes **tā yŏ-lái**

always **yúng-yuǎn** (ever-far): he has always lived here **tā yúng-yuǎn djù dzài-djŏ-li** (he always live located-here)

am, is, are **shìr** (*more information under* be)

ambassador **dà-shìr** (big-courier)

ambulance **djyŏu-hù-chō** (save-nursing-vehicle)

ambush, to ambush **mái-fu** (bury-ambush)

America, United States **Mŏi-gwə**: American **Mŏi-gwə-də** (America-belonging); an American **Mŏi-gwə-rén** (America-person)

ammunition **dàn-yàu** (shall-medicine)

amount **shù-mu** (number-index); large amount **hěn-dwō** (very-much); small amount **hěn-shǎu** (very-little)

ampere **ān-pěi** (like English): five amperes **wǔ-ān-pěi**

amplifier, loud speaker **fàng-dà-chì** (let-big-device)

and **gēn** (*same as* with): you and I **wǒ gēn-nǐ** (I with-you)

anesthetic **má-yàu** (numb-medicine)

angle, corner **djyǎu** (*sounds like* foot): right angle **djír-djyǎu** (straight-angle)

angry **shēng-chì-lə** (born-steam-done)

angular measure **djyǎu-dù** (angle-degree)

animal **dùng-wu** (move-thing)

Annam, Indo-China **Ān-nán** (safe-south)

annoy **má-fan**

answer **hwéi-dá** (return-answer)

antenna **tyān-shyàn** (sky-wire)

any (*omitted in questions*): are there any people here? **djè-li yǒu-məi-yǒu rén** (here have-haven't person)

any at all **swéi-byàn** (according-convenience): anyone at all can come **swéi-byàn nǎ-yí-gə rén dōu kě-yi lái** (according-convenience which person all allowed come)

apple **píng-gwǒ** (apple-fruit)

approximately **chà-bu-dwō** (difference-not-much)

are, is, am, be **shìr** (*more information under* be)

arm **gē-bəi**

armature **dyàn-shū** (electric-core)

armored forces **djwāng-djyǎ bù-dwèi** (install-shell section-team)

arms, fire-arms **chyāng-pàu** (gun-cannon)

army **lù-djyūn** (mainland-army)

around **ràu-dj**: he goes around the tree **tā ràu-dj shù dzǒu** (he around tree walk)

arrange (put things in order) **djéng-lǐ**

arrange for, make arrangements **chóu-bèi** (plan-prepare)

arrest **djwə̌-chi-lai** (arrest-up-come): arrest him **bǎ-tā djwə̌-
chi-lai** (take-him arrest)

arrive, reach **dàu**

artillery, artilleryman **pàu-bīng** (cannon-soldier)

artillery piece **pàu**

as, equally **yí-yàng** (one-manner): you're as good as I
nǐ gə̄n-wə̌ yí-yàng hǎu (you with-me one-manner good)

ashamed **tsán-kwə̀i**

ashes **hwə̄i**

Asia **Yà-djəu** (Ya-continent)

ask for, beg **yǎu** (*also* want): go ask for food **chyù yǎu-fàn**
(go ask-food), he asks me for money **tā wə̀n-wə̌ yǎu-chyán**
(he inquire-me ask-money)

ask, inquire **wə̀n**: he asks if it's so **tā wə̀n shìr-bu-shìr** (he
inquire be-not-be)

asleep **shwə̀i-djáu-lə** (sleep-attain-done)

assemble, get together **djyù-hwə̀i** (assemble-meet)

assemble, put together (machine parts) **pə̀i-hə́** (mate-
together): assemble that machine **bǎ-nà-gə dji-chǐ pə̀i-hə́-
chi-lai** (take-that machine assemble-up-come)

assorted, mixed **shír-djǐn-də** (ten-variety-belonging)

at, located at **dzài**: he's at that place **tā dzài-nà-gə-dì-fang**
(him located-that-place)

Atlantic Ocean **Dà-shī-yang** (Big-west-ocean)

attack **gūng-dji** (offensive-strike)

Australia **Àu-djeu** (Au-continent)

automatic **dzìr-dùng-də** (self-move-belonging)

automobile **chì-chə̄** (gas-vehicle)

autumn **chyə̄u-tyan**

awake **shǐng-lə** (awake-done): is he awake? **tā shǐng-lə
mə́i-yǒu** (he wake-done haven't)

ax **fǔ-dz**

axle, pivot, axis **djə́u**

B

back (of person or animal) **bèi**

back of, behind **hèu-byan** (rear-side): backdoor **hèu-mén** (rear-door)

back again, to return **hwéi**: come back **hwéi-lai** (return-come)

bad, no good **bù-hǎu** (not-good)

bad, in bad shape, spoiled **hwài-lə**

badge, insignia **hwèi-djāng**

bag, sack **kǒu-dài** (mouth-bag): one bagful **yí-dài**, three bags of rice **sān-dài mǐ** (three-bag rice)

baggage **shíng-li**

bake **kǎu**

bakelite, plastic **djyǎu-mù** (glue-wood)

balance remaining **djyé-tswén** (conclude-remain)

balanced account **djyé-djàng** (conclude-account)

ball **chyéu**: to play ball **dǎ-chyéu** (hit-ball)

bamboo **djú-dz**

banana **shyǎng-djyāu**

band, strap **dài-dz** (*sounds like* bag)

band, orchestra **yuè-dwèi** (music-team)

bandage **bēng-dài** (taut-belt)

bandit **tǔ-fěi**

bank for money **yín-háng** (silver-firm)

bank of river **hé-àn** (river-shore): north bank **běi-àn**

barber, hairdresser **lí-fǎ-djyàng** (fix-hair-craftsman)

barber shop **lí-fǎ-dyàn** (fix-hair-shop)

bargain, cheap **pyén-yi**

  bargain sale **dà-djyǎn-djyà** (big-subtract-price)

bargain, haggle **hwán-djyà** (return-price)

barracks **yíng-fáng** (quarters-house)

barrel, tub, pail **tǔng-dz** (*also* hollow cylinder)

barrel of gun **chyǎng-gwǎn** (gun-tube); barrel of artillery
  piece **pàu-gwǎn** (cannon-tube)

base position **yuǎn-dyǎn** (origin-point)

base-plate **dí-bǎn** (bottom-board)

basket **lán-dz**

bathe, take a bath **shí-dzǎu** (wash-bath): has bathed **shǐ-lə-dzǎu** (wash-done-bath)

bathhouse, bathroom **shí-dzǎu-fáng** (wash-bath-house)

battery (for electricity) **dyàn-chír** (electric-pool)

battle **djàn-yì** (fight-service)

battlefield **djàn-chǎng** (fight-field)

bay, inlet **hǎi-wǎn** (sea-bend)

bayonet **tsìr-dāu** (stab-knife)

be, is, are, am **shìr**: I'm an American **wǒ shìr Mǒi-gwə-rən**
  (I be America-person), this is a good one **djè-gə shìr**
  hǎu-də (this be good-belonging); *not used with simple*
  adjectives: that man is big **nà-gə rén dà** (that person big),
  I'm tired **wǒ lèi-lə** (I tired)

beans **dòu-dz**

bear (animal) **shyúng**

bear, endure **shòu-kǔ** (endure-bitter)

bear a child **shēng-hái-dz** (born-child)

bear fruit **djyē-gwǒr** (produce-fruit)

beard, face hair **hú-dz**

bearing (of machine) **djóu-chéng** (axle-support)

beat, hit **dǎ**

beat, defeat **dǎ-bài** (hit-defeat)

beautiful **hǎu-kàn** (good-look)

because, because of **yīn-wəi**: because he wants to **yīn-wəi**
  tā yàu (because he want), because of him **yīn-wəi tā**

become **lə** (*tacked-on syllable*, done) *or* **dzwè** (*same as* do):
  he became sick **tā bìng-lə** (he sick-done), he became a
  mechanic **tā dzwè djì-gūng-rən** (he do mechanic)

bed **chwáng**

bedding **pǔ-gai** (spread-cover)

beef **nyǒu-ròu** (cattle-meat)

before **yǐ-chyán**: before today **djīn-tyan yǐ-chyán** (today before)

beg, ask for **yàu** (*also* want)

beggar **yàu-fàn** (ask-food)

begin, start **kāi-shǐr** (open-start)

behind **hòu-byan** (rear-side): behind me **dzài-wǒ-hòu-byan** (located-me-behind), go behind the house **dàu-fáng-dz-hòu-byan chyu** (reach-house-behind go)

believe, trust **shìn**: I believe you **wǒ shìn-nǐ**, I don't believe what he says **tā-shwō-də wǒ bú-shìn** (he-speak-belonging I not-believe)

bell **djūng** (*also* clock)

belly **dù-dz**

belong **də** (*tacked-on syllable*, belonging): this one belongs to me **djè-gə shìr wǒ-də** (this be me-belonging)

below **dǐ-shya** (bottom-down): go below **dàu-dǐ-shya chyù** (reach-below go)

belt, strap, tape **dài-dz** (*sounds like* bag): cartridge belt **dzǐr-dàn-dài**, waist belt **yāu-dai**

bend, to bend **wān**

best **dzwòi-hǎu** (most-good)

better **hǎu-yi-dyar** (good-one-bit)

between **djir-djyǎn** (between-space): between you and him **dzài-nǐ gēn-tā djir-djyǎn** (located-you with-him between-space)

bicycle **dzìr-shíng-chē** (self-move-vehicle)

big **dà**

bigger **dà-yi-dyar** (big-one-bit)

biggest **dzwòi-dà** (most-big)

bill, statement **djàng-dān-dz** (account-list)

bill, banknote **chyǎn-pyǎu-dz** (money-ticket)

bird **nyǎu** *or* **nyǎur**

birthday **shēng-rìr** (born-day)

bite **yǎu**

bitter **kǔ**

black, dark **hēi**

blackboard **hēi-bǎn**

blade **dāu-pyǎn** (knife-sheet)

blade of saw **djyù-tyǎu** (saw-strip)

blame **gwài**: blame him **gwài-tā**, he's to blame for this matter **djè-gə shìr-ching gwài-tā** (this matter blame-him)

blanket **tǎn-dz**

bleed **lyǒu-shyǒ** (flow-blood)

blister **pàu** (*also* bubble)

block, lump **kwài**: iron block **tyǒ-kwài**, wood block **mù-kwài**, a block of ice **yǐ-kwài bǐng** (one-lump ice)

blood **shyǒ**

bloom, blossom **kāi-hwā** (open-flower)

blow breath, puff **chwēi**

blow (wind), windy **yǒu-fēng** (have-wind)

blue **lán**

bluff, cliff **shyuǎn-yái**

blunt, dull **dùn**

boards **bǎn-dz**

boat, ship **chwán**

body **shēn-ti**: vehicle body **chē-shēn**

boil, sore **chwāng** (*sounds like* window)

boil (food) **djǔ**; boil (water) **kāi** (*sounds like* open); boiling water **kāi-shwǒi**, boiled water for drinking **lyáng-kāi-shwǒi** (cool-boil-water)

bolt **lwè-sir** (spiral-strand)

bomb **djà-dàn** (explode-shell), to bomb **hūng-djà** (bombardment-explode) bomber plane **hŭng-djà-djî** (bombardment-explode-machine)

bone **gú-təu** (bone-head)

book **shū**

bookkeeper **gwăn-djàng-də** (manage-account-belonging)

born **shēng**: I was born in Shanghai **wə̆ shēng dzài-Shànghăi** (I born located-Shanghai)

borrow **djyə̀**: I want to borrow money from you **wə̆ yău gən-nĭ djyə̀-chyán** (I want with-you borrow-money)

boss, foreman **gŭng-tə́u** (work-head)

both **də̄u** (*same as* all): they are both well **tă-mən lyăng-gə də̄u-hău** (they two all-good)

bother, disturb **má-fan**: don't bother him **byə̀ má-fan-ta**

bottle **píng-dz**: a bottle of wine **yì-píng djyə̆u** (one-bottle wine)

bottom **dĭ**

boundary **gwə́-djyə̀** (country-border)

bow (with joined hands) **dzwə̀-yî** (make-bow); bow low **djyú-gūng** (bend-torso); bow and nod **dyăn-tə́u** (nod-head)

bowl **wăn**: a bowl of rice **yì-wăn fàn** (one-bowl rice)

bowling, to bowl **pău-chyə̆u** (cast-ball)

box (large) **shyăng-dz** (*also* trunk, suitcase); small box **hə́-dz**: three boxes of books **sān-shyăng shū** (three-case book), three boxes of matches **sān-hə́ yáng-hwə̆** (three-box match)

boy **nán-hăi-dz** (male-child)

brakes **shā-chə̄** (brake-vehicle)

branch **shù-djir-dz** (tree-branch)

branch office **fə̄n-háng** (division-firm)

brass **hwáng-túng** (yellow-copper)

brave **yúng-găn**

bread **myàn-bāu** (flour-package)

break by bending **djyuə̆-dwàn** (bend-snap): break into a

few pieces **dǎ-pwə̀** (hit-break), break up, shatter, smash **dǎ-swə̀i** (hit-fragments)

break down, get out of order **hwài-lə** (*same as* spoiled)

breakfast **dzǎu-fàn** (early-food)

breathe **hŭ-shi** (exhale-inhale)

bride, bridegroom **shin-rə́n** (new-person)

bridge **chyáu**

bridle, halter, reins **djyǎng-shəng**

briefcase **shŭ-bāu** (book-package)

bright, clever **tsŭng-ming**

bright, shiny **lyǎng**

bring **dài-lai** (lead-come) *or* **ná-lai** (pickup-come): bring the horses here **dài-mǎ lai** (lead-horse come), bring food **ná-fàn lai** (pickup-food come)

British Empire **Dà-yĭng-dì-gwə́** (Big-English-empire)

broad, wide **kwǎn**

broil **bāu** (*sounds like* package, wrap)

broom **sǎu-ba** (sweep-instrument, *understood everywhere but Peiping area*) *or* **sǎu-chəu** (*in Peiping area*)

brothers **shyŭng-dì**; older brother **gə̄-gə**; younger brother **dì-di**

brown **dzŭng-sə̀-də** (palm-color-belonging)

brush **shwǎ-dz**, to brush **shwǎ**

brush, Chinese writing instrument **bǐ** (*sounds like* compare)

bubble **pàu** (*sounds like* cannon)

bucket, tub, barrel **tŭng** (*also* hollow cylinder)

buffalo **shwə̌i-nyə́u** (water-cattle)

bug, insect **chúng-dz**

build, construct **dzàu**: they build a factory **tā-mən dzàu gŭng-chǎng**

bulb (electric light) **də̄ng-pàu** (lamp-bubble)

bull, ox **gŭng-nyə́u** (male-cattle)

bullet **dzǐr-dàn** (son-shell)

bunch (held together) **kǔn**, bunch, group **chyún**: a bunch of flowers **yì-kǔn hwā** (one-bunch flower), a bunch of people **yì-chyún rə́n** (one-group person)

Buddhism **fwə́-djyàu** (Buddha-teaching)

building, house **fáng-dz**; tall building **lə́u**

bump **pə̀ng**

Burma **Myǎn-dyàn**

burn **hwə́-shāng** (fire-injury)

burn, heat, roast **shāu**

burning, afire **djáu-lə**

burst **bàu-lə**

bus **gūng-gùng chì-chə̄** (public automobile)

bus stop **chì-chə̄-djàn** (automobile-stop)

bushes **tsúng-shù** (group-tree)

business, commerce **mǎi-mai** (buy-sell)

busy **yǒu-shìr** (have-work)

but **kə́-shir**: I want to go but I'm not allowed to **wǒ yàu chyù kə́-shir bù-kə́-yi chyù** (I want go but not-allowed go)

butcher **mài-rə̀u-də** (sell-meat-belonging)

butcher shop **rə̀u-dyàn** (meat-shop)

butter **nyə́u-yə́u** (cow-oil) *or* **hwǎng-yə́u** (yellow-oil)

buttons **kə̀u-dz**

buy **mǎi**

by **yùng** (*same as* use) *or* **dzwə̀** (*same as* sit): he does it with a knife **tā yùng-dāu-dz dzwə̀** (he use-knife do), he comes by plane **tā dzwə̀-fə̄i-dji lái** (he sit-airplane come)

C

cabbage **bái-tsài** (white-food)

cabinet (furniture) **gwə̀i-dz**

cable, wire **shyàn** (*also* thread)

call out, shout **dà-shə̄ng djyàu** (big-sound call)

called, to call **djyàu** (*also* tell to do): what is this thing called in Chinese? **djè-gə dŭng-shi Djŭng-gwə-hwà djyàu shə́m-mə** (this thing China-words called what)

calm, collected, steady **djàn-djing**

camera **djàu-shyàng-djī** (shine-picture-machine)

camouflage **wěi-djwăng** (false-pretend)

camp, bivouac **lù-yíng** (expose-camp)

can **hwèi** (knowing how to) *or* **nə́ng** (able to) *or* **kə́-yi** (possible, maybe): he can drive a car but isn't allowed to **tā hwèi kāi chì-chē kə́-shir bù-kə́-yi kāi,** I can't lift it by myself **wǒ yí-gə-rən bù-nə́ng bǎ-ta tái-chi-lai** (I one-person not-able take-it raise-up-come), it can happen **kə́-yi chū-shìr** (possible happen)

can, container **gwàn-tə́u** (container-head): one can of **yí-gwàn,** three cans **sān-gə gwàn-tə́u** (three-item can), three cans of fruit **sān-gwàn shwěi-gwǒ** (three-container fruit)

canal **yùn-hə́** (transport-river)

candle **là** (*same as* wax)

candy **táng** (*also* sugar)

cannon, artillery piece **pàu** (*sounds like* bubble)

canteen **shwěi-hú** (water-pot, *same as* kettle)

canvas, tarpaulin **fán-bù** (sail-cloth)

cap, hat **màu-dz**

capital city **djīng-chə́ng**

capital investment **bə̌n-chyan** (root-money)

captain **shàng-wèi** (upper-companyofficer)

capture **fú-lwǒ** (*also* prisoner); capture (supplies) **fú-hwə̀** (capture-goods)

car, cart, vehicle **chē**: motor car **chì-chē** (gas-vehicle)

carburetor **chì-hwà-djī** (gas-evaporate-machine)

card **kǎ-pyàn** *or* **chyǎ-pyàn** (card-sheet): calling card **míng-pyàn** (name-sheet) cards **pŭ-kə̀-pái** (poker-domino, *but used for all kinds of playing cards*); to play cards **dá-djǐr-pái** (hit-paper-domino)

careful **shyǎu-shin** (small-heart): be careful with that gun **shyǎu-shin nà-gə chyǎng** (careful that gun)

careless **tsŭ-shin** (coarse-heart)

carpet, rug **dì-tǎn** (ground-blanket) *or* **shí-dz** (*same as* mat)

carry **ná-chyu** (pickup-go): carry a basket **ná-lán-dz chyu** (pickup-basket go)

cartridge **chyǎng-dàn** (gun-shell)

cash **shyàn-chyán** (cash-money)

casualties **shǎng-wáng** (wound-dead)

cat **mǎu**

catch, stopping pin **kə̀u** (*same as* button)

catch, capture **djwə̀**

catch hold **djwā**

catch in the air **djyə̀** (*also* accept)

Catholic **Tyǎn-djŭ-də** (Catholic-belonging): a Catholic **Tyǎn-djŭ**, Catholic church **Tyǎn-djŭ-táng** (Catholic-hall)

Catholicism **Tyǎn-djŭ-djyàu** (Catholic-teaching)

cattle (beef animal) **nyə́u**

cattle, livestock **shə̀ng-kəu** (creature-mouth)

cavalry, cavalryman **chí-bing** (straddle-soldier)

celebrate **chǐng-dju**

celebration **hwə̀i** (*also* party, meeting)

censor, inspect, censorship, inspection **djyǎn-chá** (examine-investigate)

cent **fə̀n-chyán** (division-money): five cents **wǔ-fə̀n-chyán**

center **djüng-djyǎn** (middle-space)

center of balance **djùng-shin** (weight-heart)

central **djüng-yǎng** (middle-manner)

centimeter **gūng-fə̀n** (universal-division): one centimeter **yì-gūng-fə̀n** certainly, definitely **yǐ-dìng** (one-settled)

chain **lyàn-dz**

chair **yǐ-dz**

chairman **djŭ-shí** (chief-position)

chalk **fén-bǐ** (powder-brush *or* powder-writinginstrument)

change, exchange, trade **hwàn**: changes his money **hwàn tā-də chyán**, money given in change **hwàn-chyán** (change-money)

change, small coins **lǐng-chyán** (sundry-money)

change condition **byàn-lə**: the color changes **yán-sə byàn-lə**

character, nature **shùng-djir** (nature-quality)

character, written sign **dzìr**

charge, buy on credit **shē̌**; charge account **djàng**: charge it **kāi-djàng** (open-account)

charge, attack **chŭng-fēng** (rush-spearhead)

chart, table **byǎu** (*also* watch)

chase **djwèi** (trying to catch) *or* **gǎn** (driving away)

chassis **dǐ-djyà** (bottom-frame)

cheap, low-priced **pyán-yi**

cheat **chī-pyàn**

check **djir-pyàu** (cash-ticket)

check up **kàn-yi-kan** (look-one-look): check this **kàn-yi-kan djè-gə dwèi-bu-dwèi** (look-one-look this correct-not-correct)

checkers **chí** (*also* chess *and other similar games*)

cheerful, happy **gāu-shìng** (high-spirits)

cheese **chǐ-sir** (*like English*)

chest, thorax **shyŭng**

chest, trunk, box **shyǎng-dz**

chicken **dji**: chicken meat **djī-ròu**

chief **lǐng-shyèu** (*same as* leader) *or* **djǎng-gwān** (chief-officer)

chief, most important **dzwèi-dà-də** (most big-belonging)

child **shyǎu-hái-dz** (small-child, *sounds like* small-shoe *in some parts of China*): small child, baby **shyáu shyǎu-hái-dz**

China **Djüng-gwə** (middle-country)

Chinese **Djüng-gwə-də** (China-belonging): Chinese language **Djüng-gwə-hwà**, Chinese person **Djüng-gwə-rə́n** (China-person)

chinaware, porcelain **tsîr-chǐ**

cholera **hwə̌-lwǎn**

chop (with axe) **kǎn**

chop up, mince up **dwə̀**

chopsticks **kwài-dz**

Christian **Djî-du-də** (Christ-belonging): Christian religion **Djî-du-djyàu** (Christ-teaching)

church **lǐ-bài-táng** (worship-hall)

cigarette **shyǎng-yān** (fragrant-tobacco)

cinch (harness) **dù-dài** (belly-belt)

circle **yuán-chyuān** (round-loop)

circuit **dyàn-lù** (electric-road)

citizen **shìr-mín** (city-people)

city **chə́ng**

civilian **láu-bǎi-shìng** (old-hundred-surname)

clamp **djyā-dz** (squeeze-article)

class, quality **dǒng**: first class **yì-dǒng** (one-class)

clean **gān-djing** (dry-clear)

clear, understandable **chǐng-chu** (clear-exit)

clear, unmuddied **chǐng** (*sounds like* fresh, lightweight)

clear space **kùngr**

clear the way **dǎ-kāi yì-tyáu lù** (beat-open one-strip road)

clear weather **chǐng-tyān** (fair-day)

clerk in store **hwə̌-dji** (*also* waiter); record clerk **shū-dji** (book-record)

clever, smart **tsūng-ming**

cliff, bluff **shyuán-yái**

climb **pá-shàng** (climb-up): he climbs the hill **tà pá-shàng shăn**

climb, gain altitude **shàng-shēng** (up-ascend): the airplane climbs **fēi-dji shàng-shēng**

clip (for papers) **djǐr-byə́-dz** (paper-clasp)

clip for ammunition **dàn-djyă** (bullet-case)

clippers (barber's) **lǐ-fà-də twēi-dz** (arrange-hair-belonging push-thing)

clock **djŭng** (*also* bell): clockwise **shùn djŭng-byău fāng shyàng** (along clock-watch direction-towards), counter-clockwise **făn djŭng-byău fāng-shyàng** (reverse clockwise)

close by **dzài-fù-djìn** (located-attach-near)

close (door), turn off (light) **gwăn**

cloth **bù**; woolen cloth **ní** (*sounds like* mud)

clothes **yi-shang** (clothing-garment)

cloud **yún-tsai**

club, stick **găn-dz**

club, social organization **djyù-lə̀-bù** (together-joyful-section)

clutch (on a car) **lí-hə́-chì** (apart-together-device)

coal **méi**

coast, seashore **hăi-àn** (sea-shore)

coat **shàng-yi** (upper-clothing)

code, cipher **mì-mă** (secret-figures); Morse code **dyàn-mă** (electric-figures)

coffee **kā-fēi** *or* **djyā-fēi**

coils **shyàn-chyuăn** (wire-loop)

cold **lə̆ng**

cold, catarrh, to catch cold **shăng-fēng** (injury-wind)

collar **lǐng-dz**

collect **shə̄u-djí** (gather-assemble)

college **dà-shyuə́** (big-study)

colonel **shàng-shyàu** (upper-fieldgrade)

color **yán-sə**

comb **shŭ-dz**

combat, fighting **djàn-də̀u** (fight-wrangle)

come **lái;** come back **hwə̂i-lai** (return-come); come in **djìn-lai** (enter-come); come out **chŭ-lai** (exit-come)

come together, converge **hwə̀i-hə́** (meet-together)

comfortable, relaxed **shŭ-fu**

command, to command **mìng-ling**

commanding officer **djăng-gwăn** (senior-officer)

committee **wə̆i-yuán-hwə̀i** (commission-personnel-meet)

common, ordinary **pŭ-tŭng**: the common man **pŭ-tŭng-rə́n**, that is very common in China **nà-gə dzài-djŭng-gwə hə́n-pŭ-tŭng** (that located-China very-common)

communicate, communication **tŭng-shìn** (communicate-message)

company, business house **shăng-háng** (commerce-firm)

company, guests **kə̀-rən** (courtesy-person)

company of soldiers **lyán**

compare **bĭ**: this doesn't compare with that **djə̀-gə bù-néng bĭ-nà-gə** (this not-able compare-that), compare this one with that one **bă-djə̀-gə gə̄n-nà-gə bĭ-yi-bi** (take-this with-that compare-one-compare)

compass **djĭr-nán-djə̄n** (point-south-needle)

complain, complain about **bàu-yuan** (embrace-complaint)

complete, finish **wán-lə**: he completed the work **tă dzwə̀-wán-lə shìr-lə** (he do-finish-done job-done), the job is complete **shyàn-dzài shìr dzwə̀-wán-lə** (now job do-finish-done)

compressed, to compress **yă-swə̄** (press-shrink)

concave **wà-də** (cavity-belonging)

concealment, to conceal **yĭn-bĭ** (conceal-hide)

concern, business house **shăng-háng** (commerce-firm)

concerning **dàu** (*same as* reach): concerning this matter **dàu-djə̀-gə shìr-ching** concrete **shwěi-ní** (water-mud)

condenser (electrical) **dyǎn-rúng-chì** (electric-contain-device)

cone **djwēi-tǐ** (cone-body)

Confucianism **Kúng-djyàu** (Confucius-teaching)

Confucius **Kúng-dzǐr**

connect **dyjē-chi-lai** (receive-up-come)

continent **dǎ-djēu** (big-continent)

continue **djǐ-shyù**

control, govern **kùng-djìr** (subject-govern)

control, manage (people, affairs) **gwǎn**

controls **kùng-djìr dji-gwǎn** (control machine-shut)

convenient **fāng-byan** (direction-convenience)

convex **gǔ-də** *or* **tù-də** (protrude-belonging)

cook, chef **chú-dz**

cook food **dzwě-fàn** (make-food)

cook in water, boil, stew **djǔ**

cool **lyáng**: weather is cool **tyǎn-chi lyáng-kwai** (weather cool-comfortable)

coolie **kǔ-lì** (bitter-strength, *not a respectful word and, it's sometimes more tactful to say* workman, **gūng-rən**)

copper **túng**

copy, duplicate **fù-djāng** (secondary-sheet)

copy off, make a copy **chāu**

core **tyě-shìn** (iron-heart)

corner, angle **djyǎu** (*sounds like* foot) *or* **djyuǒ**: corner of a room **wū-djyǎu** (room-angle)

corner (of streets), intersection **djyē-kǒu** (street-mouth)

corporal **shyǎ-shìr** (lower-noncom)

correct, make right **gǎi-djèng** (alter-upright)

correct, right **dwèi-lə**

cotton wadding **myán-hwa** (cotton-flower); medical cotton **yàu-myán** (medicine-cotton)

count up **shǔ**

counter-attack **făn-gŭng** (reverse-attack)

courtesy **lĭ-màu** (ceremony-manners)

country, land **dì**

country, nation **gwǝ́-djyā** (country-family)

court of law **fǎ-yuàn**

cover, lid **gài-dz**; to cover over **gài-shang** (cover-on)

cow, cattle, bull, ox **nyǝ́u**

crank **shǝ̆u-yáu-bĭng** (hand-rock-handle)

crawl **pá**

crayon **là-bĭ** (wax-brush)

crazy **fĕng-lǝ**

credentials **djǝ̀ng-shŭ** (certificate-book)

credit **shǝ̄-djàng** (charge-account) *or* **shǝ̄**: he buys on credit **tā shǝ̄-djàng** (he charge-account), he buys a hat on credit **tā shǝ̄ yĭ-dĭng màu-dz** (he charge one-top hat)

crew, personnel **rǝ́n-yuán** (person-operator)

criticize, find fault **pi-ping**

crooked, curved, bent **wăn-dǝ** (bend-belonging)

crops **djwāng-djya** (farm-plants)

cross **shír-dzìr** (ten-character—*the Chinese writing for* ten *has the shape of a cross*)

cross over **gwǝ̀**: come across **gwǝ̀-lai** (cross-come), go across **gwǝ̀-chyu** (cross-go)

cross section **dwàn-myàn** (sever-surface)

crosswise **háng**

crow **wŭ-yā**

cry, weep **kŭ**

crystal **djing-tĭ** (crystal-body)

culvert **hàn-dùng** (soak-tunnel)

cup **bǝ̆i-dz** (*also* drinking glass): a cup of coffee **yĭ-bǝ̆i kā-fǝ̆i** (one-cup coffee)

current **lyǝ́u**: electric current **dyàn-lyǝ́u**, water current **shwǝ̆i-lyǝ́u**

curve, bend **wǎn**
curved, crooked, bent **wǎn-də** (bend-belonging)
cushion, pad **dyǎn-dz**
cut **chyə̄**
cylinder (hollow) **tǔng** (*also* barrel, pail)
cylinder (solid) **yuán-djù-tǐ** (round-pillar-body)
cylinder of gas engine **chǐ-gāng** (gas-jar)

D

dam **shwǒi-djá** (water-dam)
damp, wet **shǐr** (*sounds like* army division)
dance **tyǎu-wǔ** (jump-dance)
dangerous **wǒi-shyǎn**
dark (without light) **hǝ̄i** (*same as* black): it's turned dark, become night **tyān hǝ̄i-lə** (sky dark-done)
dark-colored **shē̄n** (*same as* deep) *or* **shē̄n-yán-sə-də** (deep-color-belonging): dark red **shē̄n-húng**
daughter **nyǔ-ər** (female-son)
day **tyān** (*also* sky): one day **yǐ-tyān**
daytime **bái-tyan** (white-sky)
dead, to die **sǐr-lə**
debt **djài**
decide **djyué-dǐng** (determine-settled): he decides to go **tā djyué-dǐng chyù** (he decide go)
deck of ship **djyá-bǎn** (shell-board)
decode, decipher **fān-yi mǐ-mǎ** (translate secret-figures)
deep **shē̄n**
deer **lù** (*sounds like* road)
defeat **dǎ-bài** (hit-defeat)
defend **fáng-yù** (prevent-resist)
definite, certain **yí-dǐng** (one-settled)
degree **dù**: how many degrees? **dwǝ̄-shǎu-dù**, thirty degrees **sān-shir-dù**

delay **dǎn-wu**

dentist **yá-yî** (tooth-cure)

department, part **bù-fən** (section-division)

department store **bǎi-hwə̀-gūng-sîr** (hundred-goods-concern)

deposit, down payment, to pay down **shyǎn-fù** (first-pay)

deposit money (in bank) **tsún-chyán** (store-money)

desert **shā-mwə̀** (sand-waste)

desk **shǔ-djwə̄** (book-table)

dessert **dyǎn-shin** (dot-heart)

destroy **pwə̀-hwài** (break-spoiled)

details **shyáng-chíng** (detailed-condition)

develop, grow **fā-djǎn** (issue-extend)

develop films **shǐ-shyǎng-pyǎr** (wash-films)

diagonal line **dwə̀i-djyǎu-shyàn** (opposite-angle-line)

diagram, sketch **tú-hwà** (picture-drawing)

dial **bwə̄-hàu-pán** (shift-number-plate)

diameter **djír-djìng** (straight-distance)

diarrhea **shyə̀-dù-dz** (spill-belly)

dictionary **dzìr-dyǎn** (word-rule)

die, dead **sǐr-lə**

different **bù-yí-yàng** (not-one-manner)

differential **chā-sù-chì** (differ-speed-device)

difficult **nán**

dig **wā**

dinner at noon, lunch **wǔ-fàn** (noon-food)

dinner at night, supper **wǎn-fàn** (evening-food)

diplomat **wài-djyǎu-gwān** (outside-contact-officer)

dipper, ladle **shǎu-dz**

direct **djír-djyə̄** (straight-connect)

direction **byān** (*same as* side): go in that direction **wǎng-nà-byan dzə̌u** (towards-that-side walk)

dirt, soil **tǔ**

dirty **dzǎng-lə**

dish, plate **pǎn-dz**

discharge (employee) **kǎi-shyǎu-lə** (open-cancel-done)

discharge (weapon) **kǎi** (*same as* open)

discipline **djǐ-lyù** (orderliness-law)

disease, sickness, sick **bìng**

disinfectant **shyǎu-dú-yǎu** (erase-poison-medicine)

disorder **hùn-lwàn** (mix-confusion)

dispensary **wèi-shēn-swǒ** (guard-body-structure)

distributor (in gas-engine) **pèi-dyàn-chǐ** (match-electricity-device)

disturb **má-fan**

ditch **gōu** (*also* gully)

dive (airplane loses altitude quickly) **fǔ-chūng** (dive-rush)

dive into water **tyǎu-shwěi** (jump-water)

divide, separate **fēn-kai** (division-open)

division, part **bù-fən** (section-division)

division (army unit) **shīr** (*sounds like* wet)

do, make **dzwò** (*sounds like* sit)

dock **chwán-wǔ** (boat-wall)

doctor **yī-shəng** (heal-person)

document, papers **wén-dyàn** (document-articles)

dog **gǒu**

dollar **kwài-chyán** (lump-money): a dollar **yí-kwài-chyán** (one-lump-money), three dollars **sān-kwài-chyán**

donkey **lyú-dz**

don't **byé** *or* **bú-yàu** (not-want): don't do that **byé nà-yang** (don't that-manner), don't come **byé-lái**

door **mén** (*also* gate)

double **shwǎng-də** (pair-belonging)

down, get down from **shyà**: go down **shyà-chyu** (down-go), get down from the wagon **shyà-chē** (down-vehicle), downstairs **lóu-shyà** (building-down), we walked down-

stream **wǒ-mən shùn-dj hǒ shyǎng-shyà dzǒu** (us alongside river towards-down walk), the boat went down-
stream **chwán shyà-shwǒi dzǒu** (boat down-water go)

down payment, to pay down **shyān-fù** (first-pay)

draft of air **chǐ-lyǒu** (air-current)

draft of money **hwài-pyàu** (send-ticket)

draftsman **hwài-tú-yuán** (draw-map-personnel)

drag, tow **twǝ̄**

drain **fàng-shwǒi** (release-water): drain pipe **fàng-shwǒi-
gwǎn**, drain plug **fàng-shwǒi-sāi**

draw, paint **hwà** (*also* a picture)

dream **mǝ̀ng**, to dream **dzwǝ̀-mǝ̀ng** (make-dream)

dress, skirt **chyún-dz**

dress up **chwǎn-chi yi-shang lai** (dress-up clothes come)

drill (tool) **dzwǎn-dz**; to drill holes in **dzwǎn**

drill, do military exercises **tsāu-yǎn** (exercise-train)

drill, practice up **lyàn-shǐ** (train-practice)

drink **hǝ̄**: drink water **hǝ̄-shwǒi**, drink wine **hǝ̄-djyǒu**

drive (car, motorcycle, etc.) **kāi** (*same as* open)

drive (animals), chase away **gǎn**

driver of auto or locomotive **sîr-djî** (control-machine)

driver of wagon **gǎn-chǝ̄-də** (drive-vehicle-belonging)

driver of pack animals **twǒ-fu** (pack-fellow)

drop down **dyàu-shya-lai** (drop-down-come)

drugs, medicine **yàu**

drugstore (modern type) **yàu-fáng** (medicine-house); old-
style drugstore **yàu-tsǎr-pù** (medicine-material-store)

drum, barrel, pail **tǔng** (*same as* hollow cylinder)

drum for music **gǔ** (*sounds like* valley)

drunk, intoxicated **dzwài-lə**

dry, dried out **gān-lə**: weather is dry **tyān-chi gān-dzàu**
(weather dry-parched)

dryclean **gān-shǐ** (dry-wash)

dry-goods store **djĭng-hwə̀-pù** (Peking-goods-store) *or* **màiyĭ-lyàu-də pù-dz** (sell-clothing-material-belonging store)

duck **yā-dz**

dummy, fake **djyǎ-də**

dull, blunt **dùn**

dung **shĭr**

dust **hwə̄i-chə̀n**

duties **djĭr-wù** (duties-business)

dutiful, diligent **djĭn-dzə́** (fulfil-duty)

duty **dzə́-rə̀n** (duty-responsibility)

dyes, paints **yán-lyàu** (color-stuff)

dynamite **dài-ná-mài-tə** (*from English*)

dynamo, generator **fā-dyàn-djī** (issue-electricity-machine)

dysentery **lĭ-djī** (purge-disease)

E

each, every **mǔi-gə** (each-item): each person **mǔi-gə rə́n**, each year **mǔi-nyán**

ear **ə̌r-dəu**

earphone **tīng-tǔng** (listen-cylinder)

early **dzǎu**

earth, dirt **tǔ**

earth, land **dì**; the earth **dì-chyə́u** (earth-ball)

east **dūng**: in the east **dzài-dūng-byan** (located-east-side), towards the east **shyàng-dūng-byan** (toward-east-side)

easy **rúng-yi**

eat **chĭr**: eat meat **chĭr-rə̀u**, he has eaten **tā chĭr-lə fàn-lə** (he eat-done food-done)

education **djyàu-yu** (teach-principle)

effect, result **djyə̄-gwǒ** (yield-fruit)

egg **dàn** (*sounds like* bullet): chicken egg **djī-dàn**

eight **bā**

eighth **dì-bā-gə** (sequence-eight-item); one eighth **bā-fən-dj yî** (eight-division-derived one)

eighty **bā-shir** (eight-ten)

elbow **gə̄-bəi djə̆u-dz** (arm elbow)

elect, election **shyuán-djyŭ** (select-vote)

electricity **dyàn**: electric light **dyàn-dēng**, electric power **dyàn-lì**, electrolyte **dyàn-djyə̆-yə̀** (electricity-loosen-liquid)

elephant **shyàng** (*sounds like* towards *and* resemble)

elevation over sea level **bá-hǎi** (extract-sea): this place has an elevation of 500 meters **djə̀-li bá-hǎi wú-bǎi gŭng-chǐr** (here elevation five-hundred meter)

elevator **dyàn-tî** (electric-ladder)

embassy **dà-shír-gwǎn** (ambassador-establishment)

empire **dì-gwə́** (emperor-country)

employ, hire **gù**

employee, worker **gŭng-rən** (work-person); employee in a business **háng-yuán** (business-personnel)

empty **kŭng-də**

end, conclusion **djyə́-wə̆i** (final-tail)

end of an object **tə́ur**: front end **chyán-təu**, rear end **hə̀u-təu**

enemy country **dí-gwə́**; the enemy **dí-rə́n** (enemy-person); enemy area **dí-chyŭ**

engine, motor **fā-dùng-djî** (issue-move-machine) *or* **dji-chî** (*same as* machine)

engine driver, chauffeur **sîr-djî** (control-machine)

engineer, expert in engineering **gŭng-chə́ng-shîr** (work-distance-master)

engineer (army) **gŭng-bîng** (work-soldier)

England **Yîng-gwə** (Eng-country)

English **Yîng-gwə-də** (England-belonging): Englishman **Yîng-gwə-rən** (England-person), English language **Yîng-gwə-hwà** (England-words) enjoy, like **shǐ-hwan**; enjoys oneself **wán-də hə́n-hǎu** (play-belonging very-good): I enjoy books **wə́ shǐ-hwan shū**, we enjoy ourselves **wə̌-mən-wán-də́ hə́n-hǎu** (we-play-belonging very-good)

enlisted man, plain soldier **bīng**

envelope **shìn-fə̄ng** (letter-seal)

equal **píng-də̌ng** (level-class): you are equal to him **nǐ gə̄n-ta píng-də̌ng** (you with-him equal)

error **tswə̀-wu** (mistake-wrong)

escape **táu**

estimate **gǔ-djì**

Europe **Ə̄u-djəu** (Eu-continent)

even if **djyə̀u-shir**: even if he spoke **tā djyə̀u-shir shwə̄-hwà** (he even speak-word)

evening (after dark) **wǎn-shang** (late-on); early evening **shyà-wǔ** (*same as* afternoon)

every, each **mə̌i-gə**: everyone **mə̌i-gə-rən** (each-item-person), every day **mə̌i-tyǎn**, every year **mə̌i-nyán**

exact, accurate **djǔn-chyuə̀**: the exact amount **chyuə̀-shù** (exact-number)

exactly **chyà-chyà**

example **lì-dz** (*sounds like* chestnut); for example **lǐ-rú** (example-like)

except **chú-lə**: all except him want to come **chú-lə-tā də̌u yàu-lái** (except-him all want-come)

exchange **hwàn**

excited **hwǎng-lə**

excuse, pretext **twə̀i-twə** (push-pretext)

excuse me, I'm sorry **dwə̀i-bu-chǐ** (face-not-up)

exhaust pipe **pǎi-chǐ-gwǎn** (dispose-gas-tube)

expect **shyǎng** (*same as* think): I expect them to come **wə́-shyǎng tā-mən yàu-lái** (I-think they will-come)

expensive **gwə̀i**

expert **djwăn-djyă** (special-ist): an expert mechanic **djī-chĭ djwăn-djyă** (machine expert)

explain **djyə́-shĭr** (solve-clarify)

explode **djà**

explosives (high) **djà-yàu** (explode-medicine); low explosives **hwə́-yàu** (fire-medicine)

extra, spare **bə̀i-yung-də** (prepare-use-belonging)

eye **yăn-djing**

F

face **lyăn**

face of an object, surface **myàn**

facing, towards **shyàng** (*sounds like* like, resemble): stands facing me **shyàng-wə́ djàn-dj** (towards-me stand-remain)

factory **gŭng-chăng** (work-factory)

fake, counterfeit **djyă-də** (false-belonging)

fall of the year **chyə̄u-tyan** (autumn-day)

fall, drop **dyàu-shya-lai** (drop-down-come); fall over, topple **shwäi-dău**

false, not so **bú-shĭr** (not-be) *or* **bú-shĭr djə̄n-də** (not-be true)

false, fake **djă-də**; false, artificial **făng-dzău-də** (imitate-construct-belonging)

family **djyă** (*same as* home)

famous **yə́u-míng** (have-name)

fan **shàn-dz**, to fan **shān** (*sounds like* hill): engine fan **fə̄ng-shàn** (wind-fan)

far **yuăn**

farmer **djùng-dĭ-də** (cultivate-land-belonging) *or* **núng-rən** (farming-person)

farmland, to farm **djùng-dĭ** (cultivate-land)

fast, quick **kwài** (*also* sharp-pointed): he talks fast **tā-shwə́-**

də kwài (he-talk-belonging fast), the clock is fast **djŭng kwài** (clock fast)

fat, stout, fleshy **pàng**; fatty (nickname etc.) **pàng-dz**

fat (of meat) **féi**: fat meat **féi-rə̀u**

father **fù-chin**

fault, mistake **tswə̀-wu** *or* **tswə̀r**: it's my fault **shìr wə̌-də tswə̀r** (be me-belonging mistake)

fear, to be afraid of **pà**

feed, fodder **tsău-lyàu** (grass-grain)

feed (animals) **wə̀i**; feed (people) **gə̌i-fàn chìr** (give-food eat)

feel by touch **mwə̄**

feel a certain way **djyué-də**: I feel badly about that **yin-wəi nà-gə shìr wə̌ djyué-də bù-hău** (because that matter I feel not-good)

female **nyǚ**: female person **nyǚ-rən**; female (of animals) **mŭ-də** (female-belonging)

fence, wall **chyáng**; wire fence **tyə̌-sîr-wǎng** (iron-strand-net); woven bamboo fence **djú-lí-ba** (bamboo-hedge)

fender, mudguard **ní-hù-dz** (mud-guard-thing)

ferry **dù-chwán** (ford-boat)

feverish **fā-shāu** (issue-burn *or* issue-fever)

few, a small number **shău-shù-də** (little-number-belonging); a few, several **djĭ-gə** (*also used for* how many)

field, open area **kŭng-chăng** (empty-field): airfield **fə̄i-dji-chăng** (fly-machine-field)

field, cultivated land **tyán**

fifth **dì-wŭ-gə** (sequence-five-item), one fifth **wŭ-fə̄n-dj yi** (five-division-derived one)

fifty **wŭ-shir** (five-ten)

fight a battle **dǎ-djàng** (hit-combat); fight, brawl **dǎ-djyà** (hit-frame)

figure, shape **yàng-dz**; figure, build (of a person) **shə̄n-tsái** (body-style) figure out **shyǎng-chu-lai** (think-out-come): he can't figure out a plan **tā shyǎng-bu-chǔ yí-gə djì-hwa lai** (he think-not-out one plan come)

figure up **swàn-chu-lai** (calculate-out-come): he figures up the amount **tā bǎ-shù-mu swàn-chu-lai** (he take-amount figure-out-come)

file for records **dǎng-àn** (section-records)

file (steel tool) **tswè-dz**

fill up **djwāng-mǎn** (fill-full)

filling station **chì-yóu-djàn** (gas-oil-station)

film roll **djyǎu-djyuǎn** (glue-roll); flat film **djyǎu-pyàn** (glue-card)

films, movies **dyàn-yǐng** (electric-shadow)

filter **lyù-chì** (strain-device): oil filter **lyù-yóu-chì** (strain-oil-device), radio filter **lyù-bwè-chì** (strain-wave-device)

find **djǎu-dàu** (seek-reach) or **djǎu-djáu-lə**

finely ground **shì**

finger **shǒu-djǐr-təu** (hand-point-end)

finish school, graduate **bì-yè**

finish up **wán-lə** (finish-done): I finished the work **wǒ dzwè-wán-lə shìr-lə** (I do-finish-done job-done), I finished digging **wǒ wā-wán-lə** (I dig-finish-done)

fins **hwá-shwǒi** (slide-water)

fire, flames **hwǒ**: to set fire **fàng-hwǒ** (letgo-fire)

fire, discharge (firearms) **kāi** (*same as* open); to fire (employee) **kāi-shyǎu-lə** (open-cancel-done); he fired a gun **tā kāi-chyǎng** (him open-gun), he fired me **tā bá-wǒ kāi-shyǎu-lə** (he take-me open-cancel-done)

firearm **chyǎng-pàu** (gun-cannon)

first-aid **djyòu-djí** (help-haste)

first one **dì-yí-gə** (sequence-one-item); first of all **shyān**: we'll tell the first one first **wǒ-mən shyān gàu-su dì-yí-gə rén** (we first inform sequence-one-item person) fish **yú**: to fish **dǎ-yú** (hit-fish)

fit (machine parts) together **pèi-hǒ** (mate-together)

fix up, rebuild **shyōu-li**; fix, mend **bǔ-yi-bu** (patch-one-patch)

flag **chí-dz**

flames **hwǒ-myáu** (fire-sprouts)

flash **shǎn-gwǎng** (lighting-illumination)

flashlight **shǒu-dyàn-tǔng** (hand-electric-cylinder)

flat, level, smooth **píng-də**

flexible **nóng-wǎn-də** (able-bend-belonging)

float, be afloat **pyǎu**

floor **dì** (*also* ground)

floor, story **tsóng**: one floor **yì-tsóng**

flour **myàn-fǒn** (flour-powder)

flow **lyóu**

flower **hwǎ**

fly (insect) **tsǎng-ying** (darkblue-fly)

fly thru the air **fōi**: flywheel **fōi-lún**

focus **djyǎu-dyǎn** (scorched-point)

fog, mist **wù**

follow **gōn-swói** or **gōn** (*also* with): follow me **gōn-wǒ**

food, meal **fàn** (*this word refers mainly to rice and wheat foods*); food-dish of meat or vegetables **tsài**

fool, deceive, trick **shàng-dàng** (up-pawnshop)

fool, idiot **shǎ-dz**

foolish **shǎ**

foot **djyǎu** (*sounds like* angle): footprints **djyǎu-yìn** or **djyǎu-yòr**

foot of measure **yǐng-chǐr** (English-lengthmeasure), *but the metric system is better known, so use centimeters and meters*

for **gǒi** (*same as* give): do it for him **gǒi-tā dzwò** (give-him do)

for, in favor of, agree with **dzàn-chóng**

force, strength **lì-chi** (strength-air)

force, violence **wŭ-lĭ** (military-strength)

force to do **yă-pwə** (press-persecute)

ford in stream **tú-shə̀-chăng** (barefoot-wade-field)

foreign **wài-gwə-də** (outside-country-belonging)

foreigner **wài-gwə-rə́n** (outside-country-person)

forest **shù-lín-dz** (tree-forest)

forget **wàng-lə**: don't forget **byə́-wàng-lə**

forgive, pardon **ráu-shù**

fork **chă-dz**

form, shape **yàng-dz** (*also* sample, kind)

form into **dzàu-chə́ng** (build-convert)

Formosa **Tái-wăn**

fort **dyău-bău** (bastion-castle)

fortification **gŭng-shĭr** (work-job)

forty **sìr-shir** (four-ten)

forward **shyàng-chyán** (towards-front)

fountain **chyuán-shwə́i** (spring-water)

fountain pen **dzìr-lái-shwə́i-bĭ** (self-come-liquid-brush)

four **sìr**

fourth **dì-sìr-gə** (sequence-four-item), one fourth **sìr-fə̂n-dj yĭ** (four-division-derived one)

frame, rack, shelf **djyà-dz**

France **Fà-gwə**

free, having freedom **dzìr-yə́u**

free, gratis **myăn-fə̀i** (exempt-expense)

freeze, turn to ice **dùng-bing-lə** (solidify-ice-done); freeze up, become solid **dùng-chi-lai** (solidify-up-come)

French **Fà-gwə-də** (France-belonging): French language **Fà-gwə-hwà** (France-words), Frenchman **Fà-gwə-rən** (France-person)

frequency **pín-lyù** (frequent-rate)

fresh **shĭn-shyan** (new-fresh)

friction **mwə́-tsă-lĭ** (grind-rub-force)

Friday **lǐ-bài-wǔ** (week-five)

friend **péng-yəu**

from **tsúng**: from here **tsúng-djə̀-li**, from now on **tsúng-shyàn-dzài-chǐ** (from-now-up)

front **chyán**: in front of the house **dzài-fáng-dz chyán-byan** (located-house front-side), go in front of the house **dàu-fáng-dz chyán-byan chyù** (reach-house front-side go), front wheel **chyán-lún**, battle front **chyán-shyàn** (front-line)

frost **shwāng**

fruit **shwéi-gwǒ** (water-fruit)

fry **djyǎn**; fry in deep fat **djá**

fuel **rán-lyàu** (burn-stuff)

full **mǎn**

fur **máu** (*also* body-hair, wool)

furniture **djwə̄-yǐ** (table-chair)

fuse, circuit breaker **báu-shyǎn-sir** (protect-danger-strand); fuse for blasting **dàu-hwǒ-swə̄** (conduct-fire-cord)

fuselage **djī-shə̄n** (machine-body)

future, in the future **djyāng-lái** (will-come)

G

gage, meter, chart **byǎu** (*also* watch)

game, contest **yǒu-shì** (mobile-drama)

garden **yuàn-dz**

garrison **djù-djyūn** (reside-army)

gas, vapor, air **chì**: poison gas **dú-chì**, tear gas **tswə̄i-lə̀i dú-chì** (hurry-tears poison-gas)

gasket, washer **dyàn-chyuǎn** (pad-loop)

gasoline **chì-yǒu** (gas-oil)

gas station **chì-yǒu-djàn** (gas-oil-station)

gate **mén** (*also* door)

gather **shə̄u-djí** (gather-assemble)

gear-wheel **chǐr-lún** (tooth wheel)

general in the army **djyǎng-gwan** (general-officer)

general store **dzǎ-hwə-pù** (sundry-goods-store) *or* **yáng-hwə-pù** (foreign-goods-store)

generally, usually **pǔ-tŭng** (*same as* common, ordinary): he generally lives in the city **tā pǔ-tŭng djù dzài-chə́ng-li** (him ordinary live located-city-in)

generator, dynamo **fǎ-dyàn-djì** (issue-electricity-machine)

gentlemen (*for addressing an audience*) **djŭ-wə̀i** (all-respected)

geography **dǐ-lǐ** (land-arrange)

Germany **Də́-gwə**: German **Də́-gwə-də** (Germany-belonging), German language **Də́-gwə-hwǎ** (Germany-words), German person **Də́-gwə-rən** (Germany-person)

get, become **lə** (*tacked on-syllable*, done): get sick **bǐng-lə** (sick-done), get well **hǎu-lə** (good-done), get soft **rwǎn-lə** (soft-done)

get, obtain **də́-dau** (obtain-reach); get, receive, accept **shə̄u-dàu** (collect-reach)

get away, escape **tǎu-lə**

get off **shyǎ** (*same as* down): get off a horse **shyǎ-mǎ** (down-horse), get off a vehicle **shyǎ-chə̄** (down-vehicle)

get on **shǎng** (*same as* up): get on a horse **shǎng-mǎ**

get up **chǐ-lai** (rise-come)

ghost **gwǒi**

gift **lǐ-wu** (polite-thing)

girl, young woman, Miss **shyáu-djyə** (small-sister); girl child **nyǔ-hǎi-dz** (female-child)

give **gǒi**

give up, surrender **tə́u-shyáng** (bow-submit)

glad, happy **gāu-shìng** (high-spirits)

glass container **bə̄i-dz** (*same as* cup): a glass of water **yǐ-bə̄i shwǒi** (one-cup water) glass material, plate glass **bwǝ-li**

glasses, specs **yǎn-djing** (eye-lens); distance glasses, telescope **wàng-yuǎn-djìng** (gaze-far-lens)

glider **hwǎ-shyáng-dji** (slide-soar-machine)

gloves **shǒu-tàu** (hand-sheath)

glue **djyǎu** (*sounds like* teach)

glycerin **gān-yǒu** (sweet-oil)

go **chyù**: go away **dzǒu-chyu** (leave-go), go back **hwéi-chyu** (return-go), go in **djìn-chyu** (enter-go), go out **chū-chyu** (exit-go)

go on, continue **djì-shyù**

goat, sheep **yáng** (*sounds like* ocean)

God **Shàng-dì** (Upper-emperor) *or* **Tyǎn-djǔ** (Heaven-master)

going to, shall, will **yàu** (*same as* want): it's going to rain **yàu shyà-yǔ** (want down-rain)

gold **djìn-dz**

good, satisfactory, O.K. **hǎu**: good-looking **hǎu-kàn** (good-look)

good-by, so long **dzài-djyàn** (again-see)

goods, merchandise **dūng-shi** (*same as* things) *or* **hwǒ-wu**

government **djèng-fǔ** (govern-residence)

governor **shěng-djǔ-shí** (state-chairman)

gown **cháng-shān** (long-robe); padded or lined gown **páu-dz**

grade, class, quality **děng**: first quality **yi-děng** (one-class)

grade in school **djí**: first grade in school **yi-djí** (one-grade)

grain **gǔ-dz**

gram **gūng-fēn** (universal-division): a gram of gold **yì-gūng-fən djin-dz** (one-gram gold)

grandchild **sūn-dz**

grandfather **dzǔ-fù**

grandmother **dzú-mǔ**

graphite **shír-mwǒ** (stone-ink)

grass **tsău** (*also* hay, straw)

grave, tomb **fə́n**

graveyard **fə́n-chăng** (grave-field)

gravel **swə̀i-shír-təu** (broken-stone-head)

gray **hwə̄i-də**

grease, oil **yə́u**

great **dà** (*same as* big)

green, unripe **chîng-də**

green-colored **lyǔ-də**

greeting **djǐng-lǐ** (*also* salute)

grenade (hand) **shə̆u-lyə́u-dàn** (hand-pomegranate-shell)

grind, sharpen **mwə́**

grind up **mwə̀**

grindstone **shā-lún** (sand-wheel) *or* **mwə̀-dz**

grocery store **dzá-hwə-pù** (mixed-goods-shop)

groove, depression **tsău**

ground, earth **dì** (*also* floor)

ground up **mwə̀-də** (grind-belonging)

group, herd **chyún**: a group of women **yǐ-chyún nyǔ-rən** (one-group woman)

grow **djăng** *or* **djăng-dà** (grow-big)

grown-up, adult **dà-rən** (big-person)

guarantee **bău-djə̀ng** (protect-certificate)

guard, watchman, to guard **shə̆u-wə̀i** (preserve-guard); military guard **wə̀i-bĭng** (guard-soldier)

guerrilla fighters **yə́u-dji-dwə̀i** (mobile-strike-team)

guess **tsāi**

guest, visitor **kə̀-rən** (courtesy-person)

guide **lǐng-lù-də** (lead-road-belonging); to guide **lǐng-lù** (lead-road)

gully **gə̆u** (*also* ditch)

gun, small arm **chyăng**; big gun, cannon **pău**; grease gun **yə́u-chyăng**

gunpowder **hwǒ-yàu** (fire-medicine)
guts **cháng-dz**

H

habit, custom **shí-gwàn**
hacksaw **gāng-djyù** (steel-saw)
hair of body, wool **máu**; hair of head **tǒu-fa** (head-hair)
haircut **lǐ-fà** (arrange-hair)
half **bàn**: half of the butter **nyǒu-yǒu-də yí-bàn** (butter-
belonging one-half), half a bowl of milk **bàn-wǎn nyǒu-
nǎi** (half-bowl milk), half a month **bàn-gə yuə̀** (half-item
month), half past three **sān-dyǎn-bàn** (three-mark-half)
hall for meetings **táng-dz**
hallway **gwə̀-dǎur** (cross-way)
hammer **dìng-chwǒi** (nail-hammer): sledge hammer **dà-
chwǒi** (big-hammer), mallet **mù-chwǒi** (wood-hammer)
hand **shǒu**
hand over **dǐ-gəi** (transmit-give)
handcraft **shǒu-gūng-yə̀** (hand-industry)
handkerchief **shǒu-djyuǎr** (hand-finecloth) *or* **shyáu-shǒu-
djin** (small-towel)
handle, grip **bǐng** (*sounds like* cake) *or* **bǎr**
hang up **gwà-chi-lai** (hang-up-come)
hangar **fə̀i-dji-kù** (fly-machine-vault)
happen, take place **chū-shìr** (exit-matter): what happened?
chū shǒm-mə shìr (exit what matter)
happen to **pə̀ng-chyǎu** (*same as* accidentally): I happened
to remember **wǒ pə̀ng-chyǎu shyáng-chi-lai** (I acciden
tally remember)
happening, event **shìr-chíng** (matter-fact)
happy **gāu-shìng** (high-spirits)
hard, firm **yìng**
hard to do, difficult **nán**

hard, energetically **shǐr-djìn** (use-strength)

harbor **hái-kǒu** (sea-mouth)

harness **wǎn-djyù** (draw-gadget)

harvest, crops **djwāng-djya** (farm-plants); to harvest **shōu djwāng-djya** (gather crops)

hat, cap **mǎu-dz**

hate, dislike **hèn**

have **yǒu**; haven't **méi-yəu**

have to, must **yí-dìng yàu** (definitely will) *or* **dǒi**: I have to go **wǒ yí-dìng yàu-chyù** (I definitely will-go) *or* **wǒ dǒi-chyù** (I must-go)

he, him **tā** (*also* her, it)

head **tóu**: headache **tóu-tóng**

head, chief **lǐng-shyòu** (guide-sleeve); head officer **djǎng-gwān** (chief officer)

head (of livestock) **yì-pi** (one-head): three horses **sān-pi mǎ** (three-head horse)

headquarters **sìr-lìng-bù** (manage-orders-section)

healthy **shēn-ti hǎu** (body good): how's his health? **tā shēn-ti hǎu-bu-hǎu** (he body good-not-good)

hear **tīng-djyan** (listen-perceive): to hear it said **tīng-shwō** (hear-speak), I hear bells **wǒ tīng-djyan djūng** (I hear-perceive bell), I hear he's sick **wǒ tīng-shwō tā bìng-lə** (I hear-speak he sick)

heart **shīn** (*sounds like* new)

heat **rə̀** (*also* hot)

heavy **djùng** (*sounds like* cultivate, plant)

height **gāu-dù** (high-degree)

hello, how do you do **hǎu-bu-bǎu** (good-not-good) *or* **hǎu-a** (good-huh); hello (on telephone) **wǎi**; hello, hey! (calling attention) **ǎi**

helmet **gāng-kwə̀i** (steel-helmet)

help **bāng**: help me look for it **bāng-wǒ djǎu** (help-me seek), help him out **bāng-tā dzwə̀-shìr** (help-him do-work) help! **djyòu-mìng** (save-life)

helper, assistant **djù-shǒu** (aid-hand)

her, she **tā** (*same as* him, it)

here **djèr** (used around Peiping) *or* **djè-li** (this-in): come here **dàu-djè-li lái** (reach-here come), he's here **tā dzài-djè-li** (he located-here)

hernia, rupture **shàn-chì**

hers **tā-də** (her-belonging)

hey! (calling attention) **ài**

hide, skin **pí**

hide, conceal **tsáng-chi-lai** (conceal-up-come): I hide **wǒ tsáng-chi-lai**, hide him **bǎ-tā tsáng-chi-lai** (take-him hide)

high, tall **gāu**: high pressure, high tension **gāu-yā** (high-press), high test gas **gāu-dù chì-yóu** (high-degree gasoline)

high-priced, expensive **gwèi**

highway **gǔng-lù** (public-road)

hill, mountain **shān**

him, he **tā** (*same as* her, it)

hinge **hǒ-yè** (together-leaf)

hire **gù**

his, hers, its **tā-də** (him-belonging)

history **lì-shǐr**

hit, beat, whip **dǎ**; hit the mark **dǎ-djùng** (hit-spot)

hoe **chú-təu** (hoe-head)

hold, take hold **bǎ**

hold back, hold-off **lyóu-shyà** (retain-down)

hole, tunnel **dùng** (*sounds like* move); hole, vent (in machinery) **mén** (*same as* door)

hollow **kǔng-shìn** (empty-heart)

home **djyā** (*also* family): at home **dzài-djyǎ-li** (located-home-in)

honest **lǎu-shir** (honesty-solid)

honorable **gwèi** (*also* expensive), *used in polite conversation*: what is your name? **gwèi-shìng** (honorable-surname), my name's Li **bì-shìng Lǐ** (humble-surname Li), what country? **gwèi-gwó** (honorable-country), my country is Texas **bì-gwó shìr Texas** (humble-country be Texas)

hook **gōu-dz**

hook on **gōu-shang** (hook-on): hook it on **bǎ-ta gōu-shang** (take-it hook-on)

hope for **shī-wàng**: we hope that you will come **wǒ-mən shī-wàng nǐ lái** (we hope you come)

horizon **shwǒi-píng-shyàn** (water-level-line) or **dì-píng-shyàn** (land-level-line)

horizontal **píng-də** (also smooth) or **hóng-də**

horse **mǎ**: one-horsepower **yì-pi mǎ-lì** (one-head horse-power)

horseshoe **mǎ-tí-tyǒ** (horse-hoof-iron)

hose, water pipe **shwǒi-gwǎn-dz** (water-tube)

hospital **yī-yuàn** (cure-court)

host, person in charge **djǔ-rən** (master-person)

hot, warm **rə̀**; pepper-hot **là** (sounds like wax)

hotel **fàn-dyàn** (food-shop) or **lyú-gwǎn** (travel-establishment)

hour **djūng-tóu** (clock-end): an hour **yì-gə djūng-tóu** (one-item hour)

house **fáng-dz**

how? in what way? **dzǒm-mə-yàng** (how-manner); how are you? **nǐ hǎu-bu-hǎu** (you good-not-good) or **nǐ hǎu-ma** (you good-huh); how come? why? **wèi-shóm-mə** (because-what)

how about? **nə** (tacked on syllable): how about you? **nǐ-nə** (you-howabout)

how much, how many **dwō-shau** (much-little); how big? **dwō-dà** (much-big); how far? **dwō-yuǎn** (much-far)

humble **bì** (see examples under honorable)

hundred **bǎi**: a hundred men **yì-bǎi rén** (one-hundred person) hungry **yàu-chîr** (want-eat) *or* **ə̀**: I'm hungry **wǒ yàu-chîr** (I want-eat) *or* **wǒ hěn-ə̀** (I very-hungry)

hunt for, look for **djǎu**

hunt game **dǎ** (*same as* hit) *or* **dǎ-lyə̀** (hit-hunt): he hunted deer **tā dǎ-lù** (him hit-deer), he goes hunting **tā chyù dǎ-lyə̀** (he go hit-hunt)

hurry, in a hurry **tsūng-máng** (hurry-busy)

hurt, injury **shāng**; get hurt, get wounded **shə̀u-shāng** (receive injury)

hurts, is painful **tə́ng**

husband **djàng-fu** (tenfeet-fellow) *or* **shyǎn-shəng** (*same as* Mister)

I

I, me **wǒ**

ice **bîng** (*sounds like* soldier)

idea, opinion **yì-djyan** (mind-perceive)

ideals **lí-shyǎng** (principle-thought)

if **yàu-shir** (want-be, *always used with* then): give it to him if he wants it **yàu-shir tā yàu nǐ djyə̀u gěi-ta** (if he want, you then give-him)

ignition **dyàn-hwǒ** (electric-fire)

ill, illness **bìng**

imitate **mwə́-fǎng**

imitation **fǎng-dzàu-də** (imitate-construct-belonging)

immediately **yí-kàn djyə̀u** (one-look then): he went immediately **tā yí-kàn djyə̀u chyù** (he one-look then go)

important **yàu-djǐn**

in **lǐ** (*used with* located) *or* **djìn** (*same as* enter): in the house **dzài-fáng-dz-li** (located-house-in), go in **djìn-chyu** (enter-go), come in **djìn-lai** (enter-come)

inch **yîng-tsùn** (English-shortmeasure), *but centimeters* (**gūng-fēn**) *are in more general use*

including **bāu-kwə** (wrap-include)

increase **djyă-dwə̄** (add-much) *or* **djăng** (*same as* grow)

India **Yìn-du**

Indo-China, Annam **Ān-nán** (Peace-south)

Indo-Chinese **Ān-nán-də** (Annam-belonging): Indo-Chinese language **Ān-nán-hwà** (Annam-words), Indo-Chinese
person **Ān-nán-rən** (Annam-person)

industry **gŭng-yə̀** (work-industry): heavy industry **djùng
gŭng-yə̀**, light industry **chǐng gŭng-yə̀**, textile industry
fǎng-djǐr gŭng-yə̀ (spin-weave industry), hand industries
shŏu gŭng-yə̀, mining industry **kwǎng-yə̀** (mine-industry)

infantry, infantryman **bù-bǐng** (step-soldier)

infected **hǎi-chi-lai** (infect-up-come)

infection **fā-yán** (issue-inflammation)

inform, tell about **gàu-sung** *or* **gàu-su**

information **chǐng-bàu** (fact-report)

inhale, draw in **chə̄u** (*same as* suck) *or* **shǐr**

inherit **chə́ng-dji**

ink **mwə̀-shwŏi** (ink-water)

insect **chúng-dz**

insignia **hwə̄i-djăng**

inspection, censorship, to inspect **djyǎn-chá** (examine-investigate)

installments, to pay in installments **fə̄n-chĭ fù-kwǎn**
(part pay-debt)

instead of **tǐ**: go instead of me **tǐ-wŏ chyu** (instead-me go)

instructions **djǐr-shǐr** (point-reveal)

instruments **yí-chǐ** (apparatus-device)

insulation, to insulate **djyuə́-yuán** (block-connection)

insurance, to insure **báu-shyǎn** (protect-danger)

interest (on a loan) **lì-chyán** (interest-money)

interesting **yŏu-yì-sir** (have-meaning)

interpret, translate **făn-yi**

interpreter **făn-yi-yuán** (translate-personnel)

introduce (people) **djyə̀-shău**: letter of introduction **djyə̀-shău-shìn** (introduce-letter)

invite **chĭng** (*also* request, please): I invite you to eat **wə̆ chíng-nĭ chĭr-fàn** (I invite-you eat-food)

iodine tincture **dyán-djyə̆u** (iodine-wine)

iron **tyə̆**: iron foundry **tyə̆-gūng-chăng** (iron-factory)

is, am, are **shìr** (*more information under* be)

island **dău**

issue, give out **fā**

itch **yăng**: to itch **fā-yăng** (issue-itch)

J

jack for lifting **chyăn-djìn** (thousand-pounds)

jacket, coat **gwă-dz**

jail, prison **djyăn-yù**

jam, jelly **táng-djyàng** (candy-paste)

Japan **Rìr-bə̆n** (sun-origin)

Japanese **Rìr-bə̆n-də** (Japan-belonging): Japanese language **Rìr-bə̆n-hwà** (Japan-words), Japanese person **Rìr-bə̆n-rə́n** (Japan-person)

jar (large), pot **hú** (*sounds like* lake); small jar, can (for preserves) **gwăn**: a jar of fruit **yĭ-gwăn shwə́i-gwə̆** (one-container fruit)

jeep **djí-pu-chə̆** (jeep-vehicle)

Jesus **Yə̆-sū**

job, work, business **shìr** (*sounds like* be)

join a group **djyă-rù**: will you join us? **nĭ djyă-rù bù-djyă-rù wə̆-mən** (you join not-join us)

join ends, make a joint **djyə̆-chi-lai** (receive-up-come)

joke **shyău-hwa** (laugh-words)

juice **djìr**

jump **tyău**

just, exactly **gǎng-gǎng**: just right **gǎng-hǎu** (just-good),
just six o'clock **djǔn-lyǒu-dyǎn** (exact-six-mark), just
eight years old **gǎng-gǎng bā-swòi**, just now **gǎng-tsái**

K

keep in a condition **bǎu-chír**: keep this thing clean **djò-gə
yǔng-yuǎn yí-dìng-yòu gān-djìng ǎ** (this always definitely-
will clean, huh?)

keep in a place **fàng** (*same as* put): keep it in the basket
bǎ-ta fàng dzài-lán-dz-li (take-it put located-basket-in)

kettle **shwǒi-hú** (water-pot)

key **yǒu-shir**

khaki, tan **kǎ-dji-bù-sò-də** (khaki-cloth-color-belonging)

kick **tī**

kill with a weapon **shā-sǐr** (slay-dead); kill by striking
dá-sǐr (hit-dead)

kilocycle **chyǎn-djòu-bwǒ** (thousand-period-wave)

kilogram **gǔng-djìn** (universal-weightunit)

kilometer **gǔng-lǐ** (universal-mile): a kilometer **yì-gǔng-li**
(one-kilometer)

kilowatt **chyǎn-wǎ** (thousand-watt)

kind, species **djǔng**: this kind **djò-djǔng**, one kind **yì-djǔng**

kind-hearted **tsír-shàn**

king **gwǒ-wáng** (country-king)

kiss **chin-chin**

kitchen **chú-fáng** (cook-house)

Korea **gǎu-li**

Korean **gǎu-li-də** (Korea-belonging): Korean language
Gǎu-li-hwà (Korea-words), Korean person **Gǎu-li-rən**
(Korea-person)

knee **shī-gài** (knee-cover)

knife **dāu-dz** (*also* blade)

knock at the door **dǎ-mǒn** (hit-door)

knock down **dǎ-shyà** (hit-down)

knot (in rope) **djyẻ**; to tie a knot **djyẻ-chi-lai** (knot-up-come)

know (something) **djir-dau**; know (people) **rèn-shir**; know how **hwèi**: I know that **wǒ djir-dau nà-gə**, he knows me **tā rèn-shir wǒ**, he knows English **tā hwèi-shwẻ Yǐng-gwə-hwà** (he knowhow-speak English)

Kuomintang **Gwé-mín-dǎng** (Country-people-party)

L

label **byǎu-chyǎn** (mark-slip)

ladder **tī-dz**

ladle, dipper **sháu-dz**

lake **hú** (*sounds like* small pot)

lamb **shyǎu-yáng** (small-sheep): lamb meat **yáng-ròu** (sheep-meat)

lamp, light **dẽng**

land, soil **dì**

land, come to land (from air) **djyàng-lẻ**; to land (from water) **dẽng-lù** (mount-dryland)

landmark **byǎu-djìr** (mark-remember)

language **hwà** (*same as* words) *or* **wén**: English language **yǐng-gwə-hwà** (English-country-words) *or* **yǐng-wén** (English-language), Chinese language **djüng-gwə-hwà** *or* **djüng-wén**

lard **djü-yéu** (pig-grease)

last before now **shàng** (*sounds like* on, up): last month **shàng-yuè**, last time **shàng-tsìr**, last two times **shàng-lyǎng-tsìr**; last year **chyù-nyan** (go-year); last of all **dzwèi-hòu** (most-behind): the last one to come **dzwèi-hòu-lái-də yí-gə rən** (most-behind-come-belonging one person)

latch **shwǎn-dz**

late **wǎn-lə**: he came late **tā lái wǎn-lə**, it's late now **shyàn-dzài wǎn-lə** (now late)

later on **hòu-lái** (behind-come)

latrine, toilet **tsò-swò** (latrine-structure)

laugh, smile **shyàu**: laugh out loud **dà-shyàu** (big-laugh)

launder **shǐ-yī** (wash-clothes), launderer **shǐ-yī-də** (wash-clothes-belonging)

laundry **shǐ-yī-dyàn** (wash-clothes-shop) *or* **shǐ-yī-fáng** (wash-clothes-house)

law **fǎ-lyù** (rule-statute)

lawyer **lyù-shīr** (statute-scholar)

laxative **shyè-yàu** (diarrhea-medicine)

lay an egg **shyà-dàn** (down-egg)

lay down **fàng** (*same as* put)

layer **tséng**: a layer of straw **yì-tséng tsǎu** (one-layer straw)

lazy **lǎn**

lead (metal) **chyǎn** (*sounds like* thousand)

lead, take along **dài**; lead, guide to **lǐng-dàu** (guide-reach); lead, serve as leader **líng-dǎu** (guide-conduct): he led the horse **tā dài-mǎ chyu** (he lead-horse go), he led the people to the house **tā lǐng-rén dàu-fáng-dz nà-li chyu** (he guide-person reach-house there go), he led his soldiers very well **tā-líng-dǎu-bīng líng-dǎu-də hén-hǎu** (he-guide-conduct-soldier guide-conduct-belonging very-good)

leader, chief **lǐng-shyòu** (guide-sleeve)

leaf **yè** (*sounds like* night)

leaflet **chwán-dān** (transmit-bill)

leak, seep out **lòu**: the pot leaks **hú lòu-shwěi** (pot leak-water)

learn, study **shyué**

leather **pí-dz**

leave, go away **dzǒu** (*also* walk); leave alone **fàng-shǒu** (put-hand); leave behind **lyóu-shya-lə** (remain-down-done): he left the house **tā tsúng-fáng-dz dzǒu chyù** (he from-house leave-go), leave that man alone **bǎ-nà-gə-rən fàng-shǒu** (take-that-person put-hand), I left your hat **wǒ lyǒu-shya-lə nǐ-də màu-dz** (I remain-down-done you-belonging hat)

leave of absence, on vacation **fàng-djyà-lə** (put-vacation-done)

left side **dzwǒ-byan**: on the left **dzài-dzwǒ-byan** (located-left-side)

leg **twǒi**

lemon **nǐng-mǒng** (*supposed to sound like English*)

lend **djyà-gəi** (loan-give)

length **cháng-dù** (long-degree)

lens **tòu-djìng** (thru-mirror)

leprosy **má-fōng**

less **shǎu** (*same as* little, *used with* compare): I have less money than he **wǒ-də chyán bǐ-tā shǎu** (me-belonging money compare-him little); less so **méi nə̀-mə** (haven't thus): he's less clever than you **tā méi-nǐ nə̀-mə tsūng-ming** (he haven't-you thus clever)

lesson **gūng-kə̀**; one lesson **yǐ-kə̀**

let, permit **ràng**: let him do it **ràng-tā dzwə̀** (permit-him do)

let go, release **fàng-lə** (put-done); leggo! **fàng-shǒu** (put-hand)

letter, message **shìn**

letter of the alphabet **dzìr-mǔ** (wordsign-mother)

level, flat, smooth **píng-də**; spirit level **shwǒi-píng-chǐ** (water-level-device)

library **tú-shū-gwǎn** (picture-book-establishment)

lice **shǐr-dz** (*sounds like* lion)

lie, speak untruth **shwō-hwǎng** (speak-lie)

lie down **tǎng-shya** (recline-down); lying on **tǎng-dzài** (recline-located) lieutenant (first) **djŭng-wèi** (middle-companyofficer), second lieutenant **shàu-wèi** (junior-companyofficer)

life, existence **shēng-hwə** (born-alive): I've lived here all my life **wǒ yì-djír dzài-djè-li djù** (I one-straight located-here reside)

lift (small thing) **ná-chi-lai** (pickup-up-come); lift (large thing), raise bodily **tái-chi-lai;** lift, pull up (by a handle) **tí-chi-lai**

light, lamp **dēng;** light for a cigarette **hwǒ** (*same as* fire): lights in general **dēng-hwǒ** (lamp-fire)

light up, kindle **dyǎn** (*sounds like* point)

light-colored **chyǎn**

light, not dark **lyàng:** it's still light **tyān hái-lyàng** (sky still-light)

lighten **dá-shǎn** (hit-lightning)

lightning **shǎn-dyàn** (lightning-electric)

lightweight **chīng**

like, care for **shì-hwan**

like, resembling **shyàng** (*sounds like* towards): I am like you **wǒ shyàng nǐ** (I resemble you)

lime (calcium oxide) **shír-hwèi** (stone-ash)

line **shyàn** (*also* thread, wire)

line of battle **djàn-shyàn** (fight-line)

liquid **yè-tǐ** (liquid-body) *or* **shwěi** (*same as* water)

liquor **djyǒu** (*same as* wine)

list **dǎn-dz:** name list, roster **míng-dǎn**

listen, listen to **tīng:** listen to me **tīng-wǒ**

literature **wén-shyué** (literature-study)

litter, stretcher **dǎn-djyà** (yoke-frame)

little, small **shyǎu;** little, not much **shǎu;** a little bit **yì-dyǎr** *or* **yì-dyǎn** (one-mark)

live, reside, stop over **djù:** I live here **wǒ dzài-djè-li djù** (I located-here reside) livestock **shēng-kŏu** (creature-mouth)

living, alive **hwó-dj** (alive-remain)

load (gun) **djwăng dzĭr-dàn** (load cartridge); load (vehicle) **djwăng-hwò** (load-goods); one load **yì-chē** (one-vehicle): a load of hay **yĭ-chē tsău** (one-vehicle hay)

loan **djyè-kwăn** (borrow-debt); to loan, lend **djyè-gəi** (loan-give)

lock, padlock **swŏ**; to lock up **swŏ-chi-lai** (lock-up-come)

lockjaw **pwò-shāng-fēng** (break-injury-wind)

locomotive **hwŏ-chē-tóu** (fire-vehicle-head)

log **dà-mù-təu** (big-wood-head)

long **cháng** (*sounds like* taste): long in duration **chăng-djyŏu** (long-lasting), the rope is very long **shéng-dz hŏn-cháng** (rope very-long), how long a time? **dwē-djyŏu**, long time no see **háu-djyŏu bú-djyàn** (good-longtime not-see)

look, look at, watch **kàn** (*also* visit)

look for, seek **djău**

looking glass **djìng-dz**

loom **djĭr-bù-djī** (weave-cloth-machine)

loop **chyuăr** *or* **chyuăn-dz**

loose **sŭng**

lose, mislay **dyēu-lə;** lose a battle **dă-bài-lə** (hit-defeat-done); lose in a game **shū-lə;** lose time **fèi-shír-həu** (spend-time); lose money (in business) **péi-chyán** (compensate-money); lose face **dyēu-lyăn**

losses **sŭn-shĭr** (damage-loss)

loud **dà-shēng** (big-voice): speak loud **dà-shēng shwē-hwà** (big-voice speak-words)

louse **shĭr-dz** (*sounds like* lion)

love **shĭ-hwan** (*same as* like) *or* **ài**

low **dī**

lower, let down **shyà** (*also* down)

lubricate **djyā hwá-yóu** (add slide-oil)

lucky **shǐng-yùn** (blessed-fate); good luck on the road **yí-lù
pǐng-ān** (one-road safe); good luck in your work **djú-nǐ
chéng-gūng** (pray-you succeed-work)

lumber **mù-lyàu** (wood-stuff)

lump, hunk, piece **kwài**: a lump **yí-kwài** (one-piece)

lungs **fèi**

M

machine **djī-chi** (machine-device)

machine-gun **djī-gwǎn-chyǎng** (machine-shut-smallarm)

machine shop **djī-chi-chǎng** (machine-device-factory)

magnet **tsír-tyè** (magnetism-iron); electro-magnet **dyàn-
tsír-tyè**; magnetic north **tsír-djèn-bèi** (magnetism-pin-
north)

maid **lǎu-mǎ-dz** (old-servantwoman)

mail **shìn** (*same as* letters); to mail letters **djǐ-shìn**

main, principal **djǔ-yàu-də** (master-want-belonging) *or* **dà**
(*same as* big): main force **djǔ-lì** (master-power), main
road **dà-lù** (big-road), main gate **dà-mén** (big-gate)

mainland **dà-lù** (big-mainland, *sounds like* big-road)

major (army) **shàu-shyàu** (junior-fieldgrade)

make, do **dzwè** (*sounds like* sit); make, build **dzàu** (*also*
to manufacture); make to do **djyàu** (*also* tell to do);
make so **nùng**: he made this hat **tā dzwè djè-gə mǎu-dz**
(he make this hat), he made a house **tā dzàu fáng-dz** (he
build house), he made me fall **tā djyàu-wè shwāi-dǎu-lə**
(he order-me fall-down), make this clean **bǎ-djè-gə nùng-
gǎn-djing-lə** (take-this make-clean-done)

malaria **yàu-dz** (in North China) *or* **bǎi-dz** (in South China);
have malaria **fā-yàu-dz** (issue-malaria) *or* **dá-bǎi-dz** (hit
malaria)

Malay **Mǎ-lái**

male (animal) **gūng-də**; male (person) **nán-də**

man, person **rə́n**; man, male person **nán-rən** (male-person)

manage, be in charge of **gwǎn**; manage (a business), manager **djǐng-lǐ** (transact-manage)

manners, courtesy **lǐ-mǎu**

manpower **rə́n-lǐ** (person-power)

manufacture **dzǎu** (*also* build)

manure, dung **shǐr**

many, much **dwə̄**

map **dǐ-tú** (land-picture); road map **lù-shyǎn-tú** (road-line-picture)

mark **djì-hau** (copy-sign); distinguishing mark, emblem **hwə̀i-djǎng**

market **shìr-chǎng** (market-field)

married, to marry **djyə́-hūn-lə** (knit-marriage-done)

mask **djyǎ-myàn-djyù** (false-face-gadget)

mat **shǐ-dz**

mate with, match with **pə̀i**

matches **yáng-hw̌** (overseas-fire)

materials **gūng-lyǎu** (work-stuff); raw materials **yuán-lyǎu** (original-stuff)

matter, job, work **shìr** (*sounds like* be); matter, affair, circumstance **shìr-ching**

mattress **rù-dz**

maximum **dzwə̀i-dǎ** (most-big)

may, allowed to **kə́-yi** (*also* maybe): you may go there **nǐ kə́-yi dàu-nǎ-li chyu** (you allowed reach-there go)

maybe **kə́-yi** (*also* allowed); it may happen **kə́-yi chū-shìr** (maybe exit-event)

mayor **tsǔn-djǎng** (village-chief) *or* **chə́ng-djǎng** (city-chief)

me, I **w̌**

meal, food **fàn**

meal, ground grain **fə́n** (*same as* powder)

meaning **yì-sir**

measuring device **lyáng-chǐ**; to measure **lyáng**

meat **rðu**

mechanic **djî-gǔng** (machine-work)

medical science **yǐ-shyuǒ** (heal-study); medical school **yǐ-shuǒ-shyàu**; medical officer **yǐ-gwǎn** (heal-officer)

medicines **yàu** (*sounds like* want)

medium-sized **djüng-hàur-də**; medium-quality **djüng-djungr-də** (middle-middling-belonging)

meet **pðng-djyan** (collide-see)

meeting **hwði**; hold a meeting **kǎi-hwði** (open-meet)

melon **gwā**; watermelon **shî-gwa** (west-melon)

melt **rúng-hwà-lə** (dissolve-transform-done)

member (of a group) **hwði-yuǎn** (organization-personnel)

mend, patch up **bǔ-yi-bu** (mend-one-mend)

merchant **mǎi-mai-rən** (buy-sell-person) *or* **shǎng-rən** (commerce-person)

message, letter **shìn**; word-of-mouth message **shyǎu-shi**

messenger **sùng-shìn-də** (send-letter-belonging)

metal **djìn-shǔ** (gold-group)

meter, gage **byǎu** (*also* clock *and* chart)

meter (39.37 inches) **gǔng-chǐr** (universal-lengthunit): one meter **yǐ-gǔng-chǐr**

method **fá-dz**

microphone **sùng-hwà-chǐ** (send-words-device)

middle **djüng-djyǎn** (middle-space)

midnight **bàn-yð** (half-night)

midwife **shðu-shðng-də** (collect-born-belonging)

might, maybe **kǒ-yi** (*also* allowed): it might rain **kǒ-yi shyà-yǔ** (maybe down-rain)

mile **yǐng-lǐ** (English-mile); Chinese mile (about half a kilometer) **lǐ**; *the official unit is the* kilometer **gǔng-lǐ** (universal-mile)

military **djyǔn** (*same as* army): military uniform **djyǔn-yi** (army-clothing), military personnel **djyŭn-rən** (army-person), military government **djyŭn-djə̀ng-fŭ**

milk **năi**: cow's milk **nyə́u-năi**

million **yì-băi-wăn** (one-hundred-tenthousand)

mine, my **wə̌-də** (me-belonging)

mine (explosive) **dì-lə́i** (land-thunder)

mine for minerals **kwăng** (*also* ore): coal mine **mə́i-kwăng**, iron mine **tyə̌-kwăng** (*also* iron-ore)

minerals **kwăng-wu** (ore-thing)

minimum **dzwə̀i-shyău** (most-small)

minister, head of a government department **bù-djăng** (section-head)

minister, priest **djyău-shir** (teaching-person)

minus **djyăn** (*same as* subtract): five minus three is two **wŭ djyăn-sān shìr-ə̀r** (five subtract-three be-two)

minute **fə̄n-djüng** (division-clock): please wait a minute **chĭng-də̌ng yì-fə̄n-djüng** (request-wait one-division-clock)

mirror **djìng-dz**

Miss, young lady **shyáu-djyə** (small-sister): Miss Li **Lĭ-shyáu-djyə** (Li-Miss)

miss, fail to hit **dă-bŭ-djùng** (strike-not-hit); missed **mə́i-yəu dă-djùng** (haven't strike-hit)

missing, lacking, to disappear **bú-djyə̀n-lə** (not-perceive-done)

mission, purpose **dzŭng-djĭr** (main-theme)

mission (religious) **chwán-djyău** (spread-teaching, *sounds like* boat-teaching)

missionary **chwán-dău-də** (spread-reach-belonging)

missionize **chwán-dàu** (spread-reach)

mist **wù** (*also* fog)

mistake **tswə̀-wu**; to make a mistake **tswə̀-lə** (mistake-done): he made a mistake in writing **tā shyə̌-tswə̀-lə** (he write-mistake-done)

Mister, gentlemen **shyăn-shəng** (first-born, *same as* husband, teacher): Mister Li **Lĭ-shyan-shəng** (Li-Mister)

mix together **hùn-chi-lai** (mix-up-come)

mixed, assorted **shír-djĭn-də** (ten-variety-belonging)

mixture **hùn-hə́-wù** (mix-together-thing)

model, pattern **yăng-shir** (shape-form)

Mohammedanism **Hwə́i-djyàu** (Mohammedan-teaching); a Mohammedan person **Hwə́i-hwəi**

momentum **dùng-lyàng** (move-quantity)

Monday **lĭ-băi-yĭ** (week-one)

money **chyắn**

Mongolia **Mə̆ng-gu**; Mongolian language **Mə̆ng-gu-hwă** (Mongolia-words); Mongol **Mə̆ng-gu-rən** (Mongolia-person)

month **yuə̀** (*also* moon): a month **yí-gə yuə̀** (one-item month), month of January **yĭ-yuə** (One-month), Month of December **shír-ə̀r-yuə** (Twelve-month)

more so **yĭ-dyăr** (*same as* one-bit): more **dwə̆-yi-dyar** (much-one-bit), more slowly **màn-yi-dyar** (slow-one-bit)

morning **dzău-shang** (early-up)

morphine **mă-fə̆i** (*like English*)

mosquito **wə́n-dz**: mosquito bar **wə́n-djăng** (mosquito-canopy)

most of all **dzwə̀i**: most in amount **dzwə̀i-dwə̆** (most-much), highest **dzwə̀i-gău** (most-high), most of them, the majority **dà-dwə̆-shù** (big-much-number)

mother **mŭ-chin**

motor, engine **fă-dùng-djĭ** (issue-motion-machine) *or* **djĭ-chĭ** (*same as* machine)

motorcycle **ə̀r-lún-kà** (two-wheel-car)

mount (horse) **chĭ-shang** (straddle-up)

mountain **shăn** (*same as* hill) *or* **dà-shăn** (big-hill): mountain range **shăn-măi** (mountain-veins) mouse **hǎu-dz** (*also* rat)

mouth **dzwǒi**; river mouth **hǎ-kǒu**

movable **nǎng-dùng-də** (able-move-belonging)

move (change one's location) **dùng**: don't move **byǎ-dùng**

move (a thing) **bǎn**

movie **dyǎn-yǐng** (electric-shadow): movie theater **dyǎn-yǐng-yuǎn** (electric-shadow-court)

Mr., gentleman **shyǎn-shəng** (first-born, *same as* husband, teacher): Mr. Li **Lǐ-Shyan-shəng** (Li-Mister)

Mrs., lady, married woman **tǎi-tai**: Mrs. Li **Lǐ-Tai-tai** (Li-Mrs.)

much, many **dwǒ**

mud **ní** (*sounds like* wool cloth)

muffler, silencer **shyǎu-shǎng-chǐ** (lessen-noise-device)

mule **lwǎ-dz**

museum **bwǎ - wù - gwǎn** (comprehensive - thing - establishment); art museum **yǐ-shù-gwǎn** (art-craft-establish-dzǒu (me ment)

music **yǐn-yuǎ** (sound-music)

must **yí-dìng yǎu** (definitely will) *or* **dǒi**: I must go **wǒ yí-dìng yǎu-dzǒu** (me definitely will leave) *or* **wǒ dǒi-dzǒu**

mutiny **bìng-byǎn** (soldier-mutiny)

muzzle **pǎu-kǒu** (cannon-mouth) *or* **chyǎng-kǒu** (smallarm-mouth)

my, mine **wǒ-də** (me-belonging)

N

nail, spike **dǐng-dz**

name **míng-dz**; family name, surname **shìng**; full name **shìng-míng** (surname-name)

narrow **djǎi**

natural, genuine **tyán-rán-də** (nature-like-belonging)

naturally, of course **dăng-rán** (right-like)

navy **hăi-djyŭn** (sea-army)

near, vicinity **fù-djìn** (attached-near): in the neighborhood **dzài-fù-djìn** (located-near), near the house **dzài-fáng-dz fù-djìn** (located-house near)

necessary, to need **shyŭ-yău** (must-want)

necktie **lĭng-dài** (neck-belt)

negative film **dĭ-pyàn** (bottom-card)

negative terminal **yìn-djí** (negative-extremity)

needle **djə̀n** (*also* pin)

neighbor **lín-djyu** (neighboring-dwell)

nerve **shə́n-djing** (spirit-fiber)

nervous, excited **hwăng-lə**

net **wăng**

neutral country **djŭng-lĭ-gwə́** (middle-stand-country)

never yet **mə́i-yə̆u-gwə** (haven't-cross), never will **yŭng-bū** (forever-not): he's never spoken **tā mə́i-yə̆u shwə̄-gwə** (he haven't speak-cross), I'll never smoke **wə́ yŭng bù-chə̄u-yān** (I forever not-suck-tobacco)

new **shìn-də**

news (published or broadcast) **shìn-wə́n** (new-hear); word-of-mouth news **shyău-shi**

newspaper **bău**

next **shyà** (*also* down): the next one **shyà-yi-gə**, next month **shyà-yuə̀**, next time **shyà-tsìr**, next two times **shyà-lyăng-tsìr**; next year **míng-nyan** (morrow-year)

nice, good **hău**

nighttime **yə̀-li** (night-in); a night **yĭ-tyān wăn-shang** (one-day late-on)

nine **djyə̆u** (*sounds like* wine)

ninety **dyjə̆u-shir** (nine-ten)

ninth **dǐ-djyǒu-gə** (sequence-nine-item); one ninth **djyǒu-fǝn-dj yi** (nine-division-derived one)

no **bū** (*same as* not, *always used with some other word*): no, it's not so **bú-shìr** (not-be), no, it's not good **bù-hǎu** (not-good), no, I don't want to **wǒ bú-yàu** (I not-want)

no, none **mǎi-yǒu** (*same as* haven't): I have no money **wǒ mǎi-yǝu chyán** (I haven't money), there is no meat **mǎi-yǝu rǝu** (haven't meat)

nobody **mǎi-rǝn** or **mǎi-yǝu-rǝn** (haven't person): nobody came **mǎi-rǝn lái**

noise, sounds **shǝng-yin**

noisy **nàu**

noodles **myàn-tyáu** (flour-strip)

noon **djüng-wǔ** (middle-noon)

north **bǒi**: in the north **dzài-bǒi-byan** (located-north-side), go north **shyàng-bǒi-byan chyù** (towards-north-side go), northern part of China **djüng-gwǝ-də bǒi-bù** (China-belonging north-section), north star **bǒi-djí-shīng** (north-extremity-star)

nose **bí-dz**

not **bū**: it's not good **bù-hǎu**, it's not here **bú-shìr dzài-djǝ-li** (not-be located-here), I do not want it **wǒ bú-yàu-ta** (I not-want-it)

notebook, pad of paper **djír-bǝn-dz** (paper-volume)

notes (jotted down) **bǐ-djì** (brush-record)

nothing **shǝm-mə dǝu bū** or **mǎi-yǝu** (what all not or haven't): nothing is good **shǝm-mə dǝu-bù-hǎu** (what all-not-good), there's nothing **shǝm-mə dǝu mǎi-yǒu** (what all haven't)

notice (announcement), to notice **djù-yì** (inject-idea)

now **shyàn-dzài** (present-located)

nozzle **lúng-tǝu** (dragon-head)

number, amount **shù-mu**

number one **yǐ-hàu** (one-numbered): room number six
  lyòu-hàu fáng-djyán (six-numbered house-space), sixth of
  May **wǔ-yuò lyòu-hàu** (Five-month six-numbered)
nurse, look after **kǎn-hu** (watch-protect)
nut for a bolt **lwó-sir-màu** (bolt-hat)
nuts **gǎn-gwǒ-dz** (dry-fruit)

O

oar **djyǎng** (*also* paddle)
obey **tǐng** (*same as* listen): obey him **tǐng tǎ-də hwà** (listen
  him-belonging words)
oblique **shyó-də**
observe **gwǎn-chá** (observe-estimate)
obstacle **djǎng-ài**
ocean **yáng** (*sounds like* goat, sheep)
o'clock **dyǎn-djüng** (mark-clock): one o'clock **yǐ-dyǎn-djung**
of **də** (*tacked on syllable*, belonging); she's the wife of a
  soldier **tǎ shìr yí-gə-bing-də tài-tai** (her be one-soldier-
  belonging wife)
off **shyà** (*same as* down): he got off the train **tǎ shyà-hwǒ-
  chə̄** (he down-train)
offer **gùng-shyàn** (supply-present)
office **bàn-gǔng-shìr** (handle-work-chamber)
officer, official **gwǎn**: army officer **djyǔn-gwǎn**, official language **gwǎn-hwà** (officer-words)
officer, policeman **djǐng-chá** (lookout-inspector)
often **cháng-cháng**
ohm **ǒu-mu** (*like English*)
oil, grease **yóu**: engine oil **djī-chì-yóu**, oil well **yóu-djǐng**
old, not new **djyòu** (*sounds like* then); old, not young **lǎu**;
  old-style, old-fashioned **lǎu-shìr-də** (old-affair-belonging)
old, years of age **swèi**: how old is he? **tǎ djǐ-swèi** (he

howmany-ageyear), ten years old **shír-swəi** (ten-age year), the car is two years old **chǐ-chə̄ shìr chyán lyǎng-nyǎn-də** (gas-cart be before two-year-belonging)

on, get on **shàng** (*also* up): on the hill **dzài-shān-shang** (located-hill-on), onto the hill **dàu-shān-shang** (reach-hill-on), he got on a horse **tā shàng-mǎ** (he up-horse), get on the wagon **shàng-chə̄** (up-vehicle)

once **yí-tsìr** (one-time)

once upon a time **yǒu-yì-tyān** (have-one-day)

one **yì** (*used with tacked-on classifiers*): one-item person **yí-gə rén** (item *for persons and things not covered by other classifiers*), one-strip road **yì-tyáu lù** (strip *for belts, straps, neckties, ropes, wires, ribbons, roads, snakes, fish*), one-sheet table **yì-djāng djwə̄-dz** (sheet *for maps, boards, tables, bedsheets, rugs*) one-stem stick **yì-gə̄n gùn-dz** (stem *for poles, posts, branches, smoking pipes, cigars, cigarettes*), one-structure house **yì-swə̌ fáng-dz** (structure *for all kinds of buildings*)

onions **yáng-tsūng** (overseas-scallion)

only **djǐr** (*sounds like* paper): only he **djǐr-yǒu tā yí-gə rén** (only-have him one person), he ate only onions **tā djǐr-chìr yáng-tsūng** (he only-eat onion)

open, not closed **kāi-də** (open-belonging); open up **kāi** (*also* turn on, start): open the door **kāi-mə́n**

opinion, idea **yì-djyan** (mind-perceive)

opium **yā-pyàn** (*like English*)

opposite side **dwèi-myàn**; opposite, reverse **shyǎng-fǎn-də** (reciprocal-reverse-belonging)

or **hə́-shir** (or-be) *or* **hái-shir** (still-be, *used in questions asking a choice of possibilities*): I want him or you **wǒ yàu tā hə́-shir nǐ**, is it one or two? **shìr yí-gə hái-shir lyǎng-gə** (be one still-be two)

oranges **chə́n-dz**

orchestra **yuə̀-dwə̀i** (music-team) *or* **gwǎn-shyán-yuə̀-dwə̀i** (pipe-string-music-team)

order, to command **mìng-ling**

order, to put in an order for **dìng**

ordinary, plain, common **pǔ-tŭng** (common-circulate)

ore **kwàng** (*also* mine)

organization, to organize **dzǔ-djir** (combine-weave)

original, originally **bə̌n-lái** (root-come)

original copy **djə̀ng-djǎng** (main-sheet)

other **byə́-də**

otherwise **bù-rán**: come earlier, otherwise you can't eat **lái dzǎu-yi-dyar, bù-rán djyə̀u bù-kə́-yi chǐr** (come early-one-bit, otherwise not-possible eat)

ought to **yǐng-gǎi**: I ought to go **wǒ yǐng-gǎi-chyù**

ounce **yìng-lyǎng** (English-tael)

our, ours **wǒ-mən-də** (us-belonging)

out, move out **chū**; outside **wài-təu** (outer-end): go out **chū-chyu** (exit-go), come out **chū-lai** (exit-come), outside the house **dzài-fáng-dz wài-təu** (located-house outside), outsider **wài-rən** (outside-person)

outline **dà-gāng** (big-maindivision)

over, to pass over **gwə̀** (*same as* to cross, pass): overdue **gwə̀-chî** (pass-date), overweight **gwə̀-djùng** (pass-heavy)

overcoat **dà-yi** (big-clothes)

owe **chyǎn**: he owes me some rice **tā chyǎn-wə mǐ** (he owe-me rice)

own, have **yǒu**

owner **djǔ-rən** (master-person)

oxygen **yǎng-chǐ** (nourish-gas)

P

pack, haversack **bə̀i-bāu** (back-wrap); animal pack **twə́-bāu** (pack-wrap); one pack, one package **yǐ-bāu** pack horse **twó-mǎ**; pack saddle **twó-ān**

pack up **bāu-chi-lai** (wrap-up-come)

Pacific Ocean **Tài-ping-yáng** (Too-level-ocean)

paddle, oar **djyǎng**; to paddle, row **hwǎ** (*sounds like* slide)

page **yè** (*same as* leaf): one page **yí-yè** (one-leaf), page-one **dì-yi-yè** (sequence-one-leaf)

pagoda **báu-tǎ**

pail, tub, barrel **tǔng** (*also* hollow cylinder)

pain **téng** (*also* hurts)

painful **téng-də** (pain-belonging)

paint (walls, surfaces) **chī**, paint (pictures) **hwà**

paints **yéu-chī** (oil-lacquer): wet paint **yéu-chī méi-gān** (oil-lacquer haven't-dry)

pair **shwǎng**: one pair **yì-shwǎng**

pajamas **shwèi-yī** (sleep-clothing)

pale **bái** (*also* white)

pan **píng-dǐ-gwē** (flat-bottom-pot)

pants **kù-dz**

paper **djǐr**

paper, newspaper **bàu**

papers, documents **wén-dyàn** (document-articles)

parachute **djyàng-lè-sǎn** (descend-fall-umbrella)

paratroops **sǎn-bīng** (umbrella-soldier)

parents **fù-mǔ** (father-mother)

park **gūng-yuán** (public-garden)

park (vehicle) **tíng** (*same as* stop)

parking lot **tíng-chē-chǎng** (stop-vehicle-field)

part, section, department **bù-fən** (section-division)

party, political faction **dǎng**

party, social affair **hwèi** (*also* celebration, meeting)

pass (way thru mountains) **shān-lù** (mountain-road) *or* **gwān** (*used in place-names*)

pass, go past **gwò** (*same as* to cross): we came past his house **wǒ-mən dzǒu-gwò tā-də fáng-dz** (we go-cross him-belonging house); in the past **gwò-chyù** (past-go)

pass to, hand to **dǐ-gəi** (transmit-give): please pass the sugar **chǐng bǎ-táng dǐ-gəi-wə** (take-sugar transmit-give-me)

paste **djyàng-dz**

path, road **lù**; path, trail **shyǎu-lù** (small-road)

pattern, model **yàng-shir** (shape-form)

pay, salary **shin-shwǒi** (firewood-water); to pay **fù-chyán** (pay-money)

peace **hǒ-píng** (harmonious-even)

peaches **táur** *or* **táu-dz**

peak **shān-dǐng** (mountain-top)

peanuts **hwā-shōng** (flower-born)

pears **lí** *or* **lí-dz**

pedal **tǎ-bǎn** (step-board)

peel, shell, rind **pí** (*same as* skin)

pen **gāng-bǐ** (steel-brush); fountain pen **dzìr-lái-shwǒi-bǐ** (self-come-liquid-brush)

pencil **chyǎn-bǐ** (lead-brush)

peninsula **bàn-dǎu** (half-island)

penis **shōng-djír-chì** (reproduction-device, *medical language*) *or* **djī-ba** (*coarse language*)

people **rǒn** (*same as* person)

pepper (black) **hú-djyāu** (foreign-peppers)

peppers (green) **là-djyāu** (hot-peppers)

per cent **bǎi-fōn-dj** (hundred-division-derived): five per cent **bǎi-fōn-dj wǔ** (hundred-division-derived five)

perhaps, maybe **kǒ-yi** (*also* allowed); perhaps he'll come **tā kǒ-yi lái** (he maybe come)

periscope **chyán-wàng-djìng** (dive-gaze-lens, *because first used in submarines*)

permit **ràng**; a permit **shyú-kǒ-djèng** (permission-certificate) person, people **rén**

personal, private **dzìr-yùng-də** (self-use-belonging); personal, individual **gə̀-rén-də** (individual-person-belonging)

personnel **rén-yuán** (person-personnel)

persuade **shwə̄-fú** (speak-obey)

philosophy **djə̄-shyuə́** (wisdom-study *or* wisdom-science)

phone, telephone **dyàn-hwà** (electric-words); to phone **dǎ-dyàn-hwà** (hit-phone)

phonograph **lyə́u-shə̄ng-djï** (retain-voice-machine)

photo **shyàng-pyǎr** (image-card)

physical training **tǐ-yù** (body-culture)

pick up (small thing) **nǎ-chi-lai** (pickup-up-come); pick up, raise (large thing) **tái-chi-lai**; pick up (by handle) **tí-chi-lai**; pick up, gather, receive **shə̄u-chi-lai**

pickax, mattock **shír-dzìr-gǎu** (cross-pick)

picture, photo **shyàng-pyǎr** (image-card)

picture, sketch **tú-hwà** (picture-drawing)

piece, lump **kwài**: a piece of cheese **yí-kwài chǐ-sir** (one-piece cheese)

pig, hog **djū**

pigeon **gə̄-dz**

pile, stack **dwə̄i**: a pile of sand **yǐ-dwə̄i shā-dz** (one-pile sand)

pills (round) **yàu-wán-dz** (medicine-sphere); flat pills, tablets **yàu-pyàn** (medicine-card)

pillow **djə̌n-tə̄u** (pillow-head)

pilot of airplane **fə̄i-shíng-yuán** (fly-procede-personnel); boat pilot **dwə̀-shǒu** (rudder-hand)

pin **djə̄n** (*also* needle); safety pin, brooch **byə́-djə̄n** (clasp-pin)

pinch **nyə̄**

pink **húng** (*same as* red) *or* **fə̌n-húng** (powder-red)

pipe, tube **gwǎn-dz**

pipe for smoking **yǎn-dǒu** (tobacco-dipper)

pistol **shǒu-chyǎng** (hand-smallarm)

pitcher **gwàn** (*also* can, tank)

pivot, axis, axle **djǒu-dz**

place, space **dì-fang** (ground-locality)

plague **shǔ-yì** (rat-pestilence)

plain, ordinary, common **pǔ-tūng** (common-circulate)

plane, airplane **fēi-djī** (fly-machine)

plans **djì-hwa** (plan-sketch); to plan **dzwò djì-hwa** (make plans); to plan to **shyǎng** (*same as* think): he plans to go **tā shyǎng-chyù** (he think-go)

plant (growing thing) **djír-wu** (plant-thing); to plant **djùng** (*sounds like* heavy)

plant, factory **gūng-chǎng** (work-factory)

plate, dish **pán-dz**; plate (flat machine part) **bǎn-dz** (*same as* board)

platform, stage **djyǎng-tái** (speech-stage); loading platform **djwǎng-shyò-tái** (load-unload-stage)

play (in the theater) **shì**; to play **wán** *or* **wár**

please **chǐng** (*same as* request): please come **chǐng-lái** (request-come); to please **djyàu gǎu-shìng** (make glad): I try to please him **wǒ yàu djyàu-ta gǎu-shìng** (I want make-him glad)

plenty **gòu-lə**

pliers **chyán-dz**

plow **lí**; to plow **gēng-dì** (plow-soil)

plug, stopper **sāi-dz**

plus **djyǎ** (*same as* add): three plus one is four **sān djyǎ-yi shìr sìr** (three add-one be four)

plywood **sān-djyǎ-bǎn** (three-pressed-board)

pneumonia **fèi-yán** (lung-inflammation)

pocket **dōur** (*in Peiping area*) *or* **dài** (*same as* bag)

point, dot **dyǎn-dz**: geographical point **dì-dyǎn** (ground-point)

point, tapered end **djyăr** *or* **djyăn-dz**

point out **djǐr-chu-lai** (point-out-come)

poison **dú** (*sounds like* read)

poke **chǔ**

poker (game) **pŭ-kə̀**

pole **găn-dz**: telephone pole **dyàn-shyàn-găn** (electric-wire-pole)

pole for carrying **byăn-dan** (flattened-yoke)

police, policeman **djǐng-chá** (lookout-inspect); military police **shyàn-bîng** (law-soldier)

police station **gŭng-ān-djyú** (public-peace-bureau)

polish shoes **shwă-shyə́** (brush-shoe); shoe polish **shyə́-yə́u** (shoe-oil)

polite **kə̀-chi**

pond, lake **hú** (*sounds like* small pot)

pontoon bridge **fú-chyáu** (float-bridge)

pool of water **shwə̌i-táng** (water-pool)

poor **chyúng**

population **rə́n-kə̌u** (person-mouth): it has a population of about one thousand **yə̌u chà-bu-dwə̄ yì-chyăn-kə̌u** (have approximately one-thousand-mouth)

porcelain, chinaware **tsír-chì**

pork **djū-rə̀u** (pig-meat)

port **hái-kə̌u** (sea-mouth)

porter **tyāu-fu** (shouldercarry-fellow)

position, location **dǐ-dyăn** (ground-point); position, situation **dǐ-wəi** (ground-situation)

positive terminal **yáng-djí** (positive-extremity)

possible **kə́-yi** (*also* maybe, allowed): I think it's possible **wə́-shyăng kə́-yi** (I-think possible)

post, pillar **djù-dz**

postage stamp **yə́u-pyàu** (mail-ticket)

postoffice **yə́u-djə̀ng-djyú** (mail-bureau)

postponed, to postpone **yán-chi** (prolong-date): we'll postpone this **wǒ-mən yàu gǒi-djǒ-gə yàn-chi** (we want give-
this prolong-date)

pot, jar **hú** (*sounds like* lake); Chinese shallow pot **gwǒ**;
deep pot **tǔng** (*same as* pail, barrel, tub)

potatoes **yáng-yù** (overseas-tuber) *or* **yáng-shān-yù** (over-
seas-mountain-tuber)

pottery, chinaware **tsǐr-chǐ** (porcelain-ware); rough, un-
glazed pottery **táu-chǐ** (earthen-ware)

pound (of weight) **bàng**, *but the official weight unit is the*
kilogram **gūng-djin** (universal-catty)

pour **dǎu** (*sounds like* reach)

powder **fǒn**: to powder (face) **chá-fǒn** (apply-powder)

powder, black powder **hǒi-yàu** (black-medicine); smokeless
powder **wú-yǎn hwǒ-yàu** (without-smoke fire-medicine)

power, strength **lǐ**: electric power **dyǎn-lǐ**, horsepower
mǎ-lǐ, one-horsepower **yǐ-pi mǎ-lǐ** (one-head horse-power),
man power **rǒn-lǐ** (person-power), water power **shwǒi-lǐ**

power plant **fā-dyǎn-chǎng** (issue-electric-factory)

practice **lyǎn-shi** (train-practice)

prepare, get ready **yù-bəi-hǎu-lə** (previously-prepare-good-
done): we'll get ready right away **wǒ-mən djyǒu yù-bəi-
hǎu-lə** (we immediately prepare), get the house ready
bǎ-fáng-dz yù-bəi-hǎu-lə (take-house prepare)

present, gift **lǐ-wu** (polite-thing)

president of a country **dǎ-dzǔng-tǔng** (big-main-control) *or*
dzǔng-tǔng; president of an organization **hwǒi-djǎng**
(organization-senior); president of a school **shyàu-djǎng**
(school-senior)

press **yǎ**

pressure **yǎ-lǐ** (press-power)

pretend **djyǎ-djwǎng**: he pretends to be a good man **tā
djyǎ-djwǎng hǎu-rǒn** (he pretend good-person), he pretends to leave **tā djyǎ-djwǎng dzǒu** (he pretend walk)

pretty **hǎu-kǎn** (good-look)

price **djyǎ-chyan** (cost-money)

priest, minister **djyǎu-shir** (teaching-person)

principal, capital investment **běn-chyan** (root-money)

principal, main **djǔ-yǎu-də** (master-want-belonging) *or* **dǎ** (*same as* big)

principle **djǔ-yǐ** (master-principle)

printing, to print **yìn-shwǎ**: print shop **yìn-shwǎ-swǒ** (print-structure)

prison, jail **djyǎn-yù**

prisoner **fǎn-rən** (violate-person); prisoner of war **fú-lwǒ** (*also* to capture)

private, personal **dzìr-yùng-də** (self-use-belonging) *or* **sìr**: private affairs **sìr-shìr**, personal letter **sìr-rén-də shìn** (private-person-belonging letter)

private (army) **ər-děng-bìng** (two-class-soldier)

probably **dwə̄-bàn** (more-half)

problem, question **wən-tǐ** (ask-subject)

produce, give forth **chū** (*same as* out, exit)

profit **djwàn**

program, plan of activity **djì-hwǎ** (plan-sketch)

promise **yún-shyǔ** (fulfil-permit)

pronunciation, to pronounce **fā-yin** (issue-sound)

proof **fáng** (*same as* prevent): water proof **fáng-shwǒi** (prevent-water), waterproof clothes **fáng-shwǒi-yi**

prop up **djìr-chi-lai** (prop-up-come)

propaganda **shyuǎn-chwán**

propeller **twə̄i-djìn-djī** (push-advance-machine)

prostitute **djì-nyǔ** (prostitute-female)

protect **bǎu-hu**

Protestant Christianity **Yə̄-sū-djyǎu** (Jesus-teaching)

protractor **lyáng-djyǎu-chì** (measure-angle-device)

province **shěng** (*also* state)

public **gūng-gùng**: public matter **gūng-shìr**

pull **lă**

pulley **hwá-chə̄** (slide-vehicle)

pump by pressure **dă** (*same as* hit); pump by suction **chə̆u** (*same as* suck): water pump **chə̆u-shwə̆i-dji** (suck-water-machine) *or* **dá-shwə̆i-dji** (hit-water-machine)

punish **chə̆ng-fá**

pure **chún**

purple **dzǐr-də** (purple-belonging)

purpose **dzŭng-djǐr** (main-theme)

purse, wallet **chyán-bău** (money-wrap)

pus **núng** *or* **nə́ng**

push **twə̆i**

put down, place **fàng** (*also* release)

put in order **djə́ng-li**

put off, postpone **yán-chi** (prolong-date)

put on (shirt, pants, socks) **chwăn**; put on (hat, gloves, shoes, eyeglasses) **dăi** (*sounds like* take along, lead)

put out, extinguish **shí**: put out fire **shí-hwə̆**, put out light **shí-də̄ng**

put together, combine **hə́-chi-lai** (together-up-come)

Q

quality **hău-hwài** (good-bad); good quality **hău** (*same as* good)

quarrel **djə̄ng-chău**

quarry **kăi-shír-təu-də dǐ-fang** (open-stone-belonging place)

quarter, one fourth **sìr-fə̄n-dj yi** (four-division-derived one); quarter of an hour **yí-kə̀-djŭng** (one-quarter-clock)

question, problem **wə̀n-tí** (ask-topic)

quick, fast **kwài**: we run fast **wə̆-mən-pău-də kwài** (we-run-belonging fast)

quiet **ăn-djing** (peace-silence)

quinine **kwə̄i-níng** (*like English*)

R

rabbit **tù-dz** (*means* homosexual *if applied to a person*)

rack, shelf **djyà-dz** (*also* frame)

radiator **sàn-rè-chì** (disperse-heat-device)

radio **wú-shyàn-dyàn** (without-wire-electricity): radio station **wú-shyàn-dyàn-tái** (radio-stage)

radius **bàn-djìng** (half-distance)

raft **mù-pái** (wood-arrangement)

rag **pwè-bù** (broken-cloth)

raid **tèu-shí** (steal-raid); air raid **kǔng-shí**

railroad **tyě-lù** (iron-road)

rain **yǔ**; it rains **shyà-yǔ** (down-rain)

raincoat **yǔ-yi** (rain-clothes)

rank (military) **djyè-dji**: what's your rank? **nǐ shìr shém-mə djyè-dji** (you be what rank)

rat **hàu-dz** (*same as* mouse) *or* **dà-hàu-dz** (big-mouse)

raw **shēng-də** (*same as* born-belonging)

razor **gwā-lyǎn-dāu** (shave-face-knife)

reach, arrive **dàu** (*sounds like* pour)

reach out **shēn-chu-chyu** (reach-out-go) *or* **shēn-chu-lai** (reach-out-come)

read **dú** (*sounds like* poison) *or* **kàn** (*same as* look at)

ready **hǎu-lə** (good-done); get ready **yù-bəi-hǎu-lə** (previously-prepare-good-done)

really **shír-dzài**

rear **hèu-təu** (back-end): rear wheels **hèu-lún** (rear-wheel)

reason **lǐ-yú**

receipt **shēu-tyáu** (collect-slip)

receive **shēu-dàu** (collect-reach)

recognize **rèn-də** (acquaint-obtain)

record (phonograph) **chàng-pyǎn** (sing-card); to make a recording **gwàn-yin** (record-sound) records (written) **djì-lù**; to record (in writing) **shyǒ-shya-lai** (write-down-come)

recruit **djäu** (*also* beckon, hail)

rectum **gäng-mǝn** (anus-door, *medical word*) *or* **pì-gu-yǎn** (rump-eye, *plain language*)

red **húng**

Red Cross **Húng-shír-dzìr-hwǝi** (red-cross-organization)

regiment **twǎn**

region **dì-fang** (*same as* place) *or* **bù-fǝn** (*same as* part)

register (at a hotel) **dǝng-djì** (register-record)

register (mail) **gwà-hàu** (hang-number)

regulations **fǎ-gwǝi** (method-rule)

reins **djyäng-shǝng** (bridle-rope)

relapsing fever **hwǝi-gwǝi-rǝ** (return-back-hot)

relatives **chìn-chi** (intimate-kinsman)

religion **dzǔng-djyǎu** (sect-teaching)

remember, keep in mind **djì-dǝ**; remember, recall **shyáng-chi-lai** (think-up-come)

rental **dzǔ-chyán** (rent-money), to rent **dzǔ**: the rent is thirty dollars a month **dzǔ-chyan shìr sǎn-shir-kwài yí-gǝ yuǝ** (rent-money be thirty-piece one month), I want to rent a house **wǒ yàu-dzǔ yì-swǒ fáng-dz** (I want-rent one-structure house), he rents to us **tä dzǔ gǝi-wǒ-mǝn** (he rent give-us)

repair, rebuild **shyǝu-li**; repair, sew up, patch up **bǔ-yi-bu** (mend-one-mend): repair the house **bǎ-fáng-dz shyǝu-li-chi-lai** (take-house rebuild-up-come), repair the shoes **bǎ-pí-shyǝ bǔ-yi-bu** (take-leather-shoe mend-one-mend)

repair shop **shyǝu-li-chǎng** (repair factory)

repellent **fáng-wǝn-yàu** (prevent-mosquito-medicine)

report, message **bàu-gàu** (report-tell)

reporter (newspaper) **djì-djǒ** (record-er)

representative, to represent **dài-byǎu**

republic **mín-gwá** (people-country)

request **chǐng** (*also* invite, please)

resemble **shyàng** (*sounds like* towards)

resistance, to resist **dǐ-kàng** (resist-withstand)

resistance (electrical) **dyàn-dzǔ** (electric-hinder)

rest up **shyǒu-shi**

restaurant **fàn-gwǎn** (food-establishment)

result, effect **djyá-gwá** (yield-fruit)

retreat **chá-twài** (remove-withdraw)

return to, give back to **hwán-gəi** (repay-give)

return to a place **hwái-chyu** (return-go) *or* **hwái-lai** (return-come)

reverse, opposite **shyàng-fǎn-də** (reciprocal-reverse-belonging)

rib bone **lá-gǔ**; rib (in machine construction) **lá-tsái** (rib-timber)

rice (raw grain) **mǐ**; cooked rice **fàn** (*same as* food) *or* **mǐ-fàn** (rice-food); young rice plants **yàng**; mature rice **dàu-dz**; unhusked grain rice **gǔ-dz**

rich, wealthy **yǒu-chyán** (have-money)

ricksha **yáng-chá** (overseas-cart)

ride (animals) **chí** (*same as* straddle); ride (vehicles) **dzwà** (*same as* sit): ride a horse **chí-mǎ** (straddle-horse), ride a car **dzwà-chì-chá** (sit-gas-vehicle)

ridge **shān-djí** (mountain-spine)

rifle, small arm **chyǎng**

right, correct **dwài-lə**; one's rights **chyuán-lǐ**

right away **yí-kàn djyàu** (one-look then): I'll be right back **wá yí-kàn djyàu hwái-lai** (I one-look then return-come)

right hand side **yàu-byan**: go right **shyàng-yàu-byan chyu** (towards-righthand-side go)

ring **chyuár** (*same as* loop)

riot **bàu-dùng** (burst-move)

ripe **shŕu** (*also* well-cooked, done)

rise up **chĭ-lai** (rise-come)

river, stream **hŕ**: river bank **hŕ-àn**

rivet **màu-dĭng** (hat-nail)

road **lù** (*also* path): main road, highway **dà-lù** (big-road), hard-surface road **yìng-myàn-lù**

roast **shău** (*same as* burn) *or* **kău** (*same as* bake)

rock, stone **shĭr-təu** (stone-head)

rocket **hwŕ-djyàn** (fire-arrow)

rod **găn-dz** (*also* stick, shaft)

roof **fáng-dĭng** (house-top)

roll over, rotate **gŭn**

roll up **djyuăn**; a roll of tape **yì-djyăn dài-dz** (one-roll tape)

roller **gŭn-dz**; roller for flattening ground **nyăn-dz**

room **wŭ-dz**; room, space **dì-fang** (*same as* place): there are three rooms in that house **nà-swə fáng-dz yŕu săn-djyăn wŭ-dz** (that-structure house have three-compartment room), there's no room **mŕi-yəu dì-fang** (haven't place)

root **gən** (*sounds like* with)

rope, string **shŕng-dz**

rotten, to rot **làn-lə**

rough (cloth, board, etc.), not smooth **tsŭ**; rough (terrain, road) **bù-píng** (not-level)

round, circular, ball-shaped **yuán**

round of ammunition **yì-fā dàn-yàu** (one-issue ammunition)

route **lù** (*same as* road)

row **pái**: a row of men **yì-pái rŕn** (one-row person)

row, paddle **hwá** (*sounds like* slide)

rub **tsā** (*also* scrape, scrub)

rubber **shyàng-pí** (elephant-skin)

rudder **dwŕ**

rug, carpet **dì-tăn** (ground-blanket) *or* **shí-dz** (*same as* mat)

ruler, straightedge **chĭr** (*also* foot of measure)

rules, regulations **fǎ-gwěi** (method-rule)

rumor **yǎu-yan**

rump **tún-bù** (rump-section, *refined language*) *or* **pì-gu** (flatus-haunch, *plain language*)

run, flow **lyǒu**

run, go fast **pǎu**

run after, chase **djwěi**

run away, escape **tǎu-dzǒu** (escape-leave)

running (machine) **kāi-dj-nə** (start-continue)

Russia **ě-gwə**

ruts **chě-dzǒu-də yìn** *or* **yěr** (vehicle-go-belonging print)

S

sack, bag **dài**; a sackful **yí-dài** (one-sack)

sad **běi-āi-də**

saddle **ān-dz**

safe, out of danger **píng-ān** (level-peace) *or* **ān-chyuǎn**: he's safe **tā píng-ān**, that place is safe now **nǎ-li ān-chyuǎn-lə** (there safe-done), it's safe to go **kǒ-yi chyù-lə** (possible go-done)

sail **fán**; to sail (boats) **kāi** (*also* drive *and* open)

salt **yán**

salute, greeting, to salute **djìng-lǐ**

salvage **lì-yùng fěi-wu** (benefit-use waste-things)

same, alike **yí-yàng** (one-manner) *or* **túng-yàng** (same-manner): this is the same as that **djě-gə gěn-nǎ-gə yí-yàng** (this with-that alike)

sample **yàng-dz** (*also* form)

sand **shā-dz**: sandbag **shā-dài**, sandpaper **shā-djǐr**, sand table **shā-pán** (sand-plate)

satisfied **mǎn-yì** (full-mind); to satisfy **ràng mǎn-yì** (allow full-mind): satisfy him **ràng-tā mǎn-yì** (allow-him full-mind)

Saturday **lǐ-bài-lyěu** (week-six)

save, keep bǎu-tsún (protect-keep)

save, avoid waste djyǒ-shǒng (reduce-spare): save time shǒng shír-həu

save, rescue djyǒu (*sounds like* then)

save face lyǒu-gə myàn-dz

saw (tool) djyù

say, speak shwǒ: he says we may come tā-shwǒ wǒ-mən kǒ-yi lái (he-speak we allowed come)

scale (for weighing) chǒng; measuring scale kǒ-dù (carve-degree); proportional scale bǐ-lì-chǐr (compare-example-ruler *or* ratio-ruler)

scalp tǒu-pí (head-skin)

school shyuǒ-shyàu (study-school)

schoolmate túng-shyuǒ-də (same-study-belonging)

scissors, shears djyǎn-dz

scrape tsǎ (*also* scrub, rub)

scratch djwǎ (*also* grasp)

screen, curtain mù

screening wire tyǒ-shǎ (iron-gauze)

screw lwǒ-sir-dǐng (spiral-strand-nail)

screwdriver gǎn-djwǒi (drive-point)

sea hǎi: seacoast hǎi-àn, seaport hái-kǒu (sea-mouth)

seal tú-djang (chart-emblem)

searchlight tàn-djàu-dǒng (seek-shine-lamp)

season djì: a season yí-djì (one-season), this season djà-yí-djì

second (of time) yì-myǎu (one-second)

second one dì-àr-gə (sequence-two-item)

secret mì-mi

secretary, clerk shū-dji (write-record)

section, department, part bù-fən (section-division)

sector dì-chyǔ (ground-area)

sedative djàn-dìng-yàu (calm-medicine)

see **kàn-djyan** (look-perceive)

seed **djǔng-dz**

seem **hǎu-shyang** (good-resemble): this seems good **djǎ-gə hǎu-shyang shìr hǎu-də** (this seem be good-belonging)

self **dzìr-djǐ**: do it yourself **nǐ dzìr-djǐ dzwò** (you self do)

sell **mài**

send (things) **sùng**; send (gifts to) **sùng-gəi** (send-give); send (people) **pài**

sentence, phrase **hwà** (*same as* words): one sentence **yí-djyù hwà** (one-phrase words)

sentry **wèi-bìng** (guard-soldier)

separate, divide **fēn-kāi** (division-open)

sergeant **djūng-shìr** (middle-noncom)

servant **yùng-rən** (use-person)

serve (food) **kāi-fàn** (open-food): dinner is served **fàn kāi-lə** (food open-done)

serve as **dzwò** (*same as* do): he served in the army **tā dzwò-bìng** (he do-soldier)

set **tàu**: a set of books **yí-tàu shǔ** (one-set book)

set off **fàng** (*same as* let go)

set the table **bǎi djwǒ-dz**

seven **chī**

seventh **dì-chī-gə** (sequence-seven-item); one seventh **chī-fēn-dj yī** (seven-division-derived one)

seventy **chī-shír** (seven-ten)

sew **fǒng**

sew up, patch up **bú-chi-lai** (patch-up-come)

sex intercourse **shìng-djyāu**; to have sex relations **fā-shēng gwǎn-shi** (happen relations)

shadow **yǐng-dz**

shaft, rod, stock **gǎn-dz**: drive-shaft **djòu-gǎn** (axle-shaft)

shake, rock **yáu**

shake hands **lā-shǒu** (pull-hand)

shallow **chyǎn** (*also* elementary)

shape, form **yàng-dz** (*also* sample, sort)

sharp-edged **djyǎn**; sharp-pointed **kwài** (*also* fast); six
o'clock sharp **djǔn-lyòu-dyǎn** (exact-six-mark)

shave **gwǎ**: shave the face gwǎ-lyǎn (shave-face)

she, her **tā** (*same as* him, it)

sheep, goat **yáng** (*sounds like* ocean)

sheet (bed) **bèi-dān** (cover-sheet)

sheet of paper **yì-djāng djǐr** (one-sheet paper)

sheet steel **gāng-pyàn** (steel-slice)

shelf, rack **djyà-dz** (*also* frame)

shell (artillery) **pàu-dàn** (cannon-shell)

shell, peel **pí** (*same as* skin) *or* **kér**

shield **gāng-bǎn** (steel-board)

shift for gears **pái-dǎng** (arrange-thwart)

shine light on **djàu** (*also* to photograph)

shine shoes **shwā-shyé** (brush-shoes)

ship, boat **chwán**

shirt **chèn-yî** (lining-clothes)

shoes **shyé** (*in North China*) *or* **hái-dz** (*in South, sounds
like* child); shoe-polish **shyé-yéu** (shoe-oil)

shoot, shoot at **shè**

shop, store **pù-dz**; to shop **mǎi-dūng-shi** (buy-things)

shop, workshop **dji-chǐ-fáng** (machine-house)

short (people) **ǎi**; short (things), low **dî**; short in length or
time **dwǎn**: short circuit **dwǎn-lù** (short-road), short
wave **dwǎn-bwō**

should, ought to **yīng-gāi**: I should go **wǒ yīng-gāi chyù**

shoulder **djyǎn-bǎng** (shoulder-wing)

shovel, spade **chǎn-dz**

show, point out **djǐr**: show it to me **djír géi-wǝ kàn** (point
give-me look)

shrapnel **lyéu-sǎn-dàn** (pomegranate-sleet-shell)

shredded bit, strand **sir** (*sounds like* silk)

shrine **myàu**

shut, close **gwǎn**

sick, sickness **bìng**; get sick **bìng-lə** (sick-done)

side, direction **byān**: one-side **yì-byān**, towards the north
  shyàng-bèi-byan (towards-north-side), on this side of the
  hill **dzài-shān djè-byan** (located-hill this-side)

sight, aim **myáu-djǔn** (sight-accurate)

sign (advertising) **djāu-pai** (beckon-board); road sign **lù-
  pái** (road-board)

signal **shìn-hàu** (message-sign)

silk **sir** (*also* strand, shred)

silly, foolish **shǎ**

silver **yín-dz**

sing **chàng-gə̄** (sing-song)

sink **chén-lə** (sink-done)

sisters **djyǒ-mèi**; older sister **djyǒ-djyə**; younger sister
  mèi-mei

sit **dzwè** (*sounds like* do, make); sit up **dzwè-chi-lai** (sit-up-
  come)

situation **chíng-kwàng** (fact-condition)

six **lyòu**

sixth **dì-lyòu-gə** (sequence-six-item); one sixth **lyòu-fēn-dj
  yì** (six-division-derived one)

sixty **lyòu-shir** (six-ten)

size **dà-shyǎu** (big-small); what size? **dwə̄-dǎ** (much-big)

sketch **yàu-tú** (essentials-picture)

skillful **shóu-lyàn-də** (ripe-exercise-belonging)

skin, hide **pí**

skinny **shòu**

skirmish **chyán-shàu-djàn** (forward-sentry-fight)

skirt **chyún-dz**

sky **tyān** (*also* day)

sled, sleigh **shyuǎ-chǒ** (snow-vehicle)

sleeping **shwài-djyàu** (sleep-slumber); to fall asleep **shwài-djáu-lə** (sleep-attain-done)

slice **pyàn** (*also* thick sheet, card): a slice **yí-pyàn** (one-slice), three slices of meat **sān-pyàn-ròu**, sliced meat **ròu-pyàn** (meat-slice)

slip (woman's undergarment) **chèn-chyún** underlayer-skirt)

slippery, to slide **hwá** (*sounds like* to paddle, row)

slope **shyá-myàn** (oblique-surface); degree of slope **shyá-dù** (oblique-degree)

slot **yǎn** (*sounds like* eye)

slow **màn**: go slow **màn-màn dzǒu** (slow-slow walk), the clock is slow **djǔng màn** (clock slow)

small **shyǎu**

smart, clever, intelligent **tsǔng-ming** (clever-bright)

smell **wén**: it smells bad **bù-hǎu wén** (not-good smell), I smell it **wǒ wén-ta**, take a smell **wén-yi-wən** (smell-one-smell)

smile, grin **shyàu** (*also* laugh)

smoke **yān** (*also* tobacco); to smoke tobacco **chǒu-yān** (suck-tobacco) *or* **chǐr-yān** (eat-tobacco, *used in the south*)

smooth, flat, level **píng**

snake **shé**

sniper **dzǔ-dji-shǒu** (swoop-strike-hand)

snow **shyuǎ**; it snows **shyà-shyuǎ** (down-snow)

so, like this **djà-yàng** (this-manner): do like this **djà-yàng dzwò** (this-manner do), don't do this **byá djà-yàng**

soak **pàu** (*sounds like* cannon *and* bubble)

soap **yí-dz** (*North and Central China*) *or* **féi-dzàu** (fat-pod)

socket for lamp **dēng-tóu** (lamp-head); tube socket **gwǎn-dzwò** (tube-seat)

socks, stockings **wà-dz**

soda water **chì-shwǒr** *or* **chì-shwǒi** (gas-water); baking soda kǎu-myàn-bāu-də sū-dǎ (bake-bread-belonging soda); washing soda shǐ-yi-shang-də sū-dǎ (wash-clothes-belonging soda)

sofa shā-fā

soft rwǎn

soldering metal hàn-shí (solder-tin); to solder, weld hàn-chi-lai (solder-up-come)

soldier bīng *or* djyǔn-rén (army-person)

solid, not hollow shír-shìn-də (honest-heart-belonging); solid, not liquid gù-tǐ (firm-body)

solve, work out djyǒ-djyué

some, not all yǒu-də (have-belonging): some people do it yǒu-də rén dzwò, some things yǒu-də dǔng-shi, sometimes yǒu-də shír-həu

something dǔng-shi (*same as* thing): he wants something tā yàu dǔng-shi

someone yǒu-rén (have-person): someone was looking for you yǒu-rən djáu-nǐ (someone seek-you)

son ér-dz

song gēr

soon kwài (*same as* fast, *used with* lə): he'll arrive soon tā kwài lái-lə (he fast come-done)

sore, boil chwāng (*sounds like* window)

sore, painful téng-də (pain-belonging)

sorry nán-shòu (hard-endure); sorry, regretful hòu-hwǒi; I'm sorry, excuse me dwòi-bu-chi (face-not-up)

soul, spirit líng-hún

sound, not defective djyàn-chyuán (healthy-whole)

sounds, noise shēng-yin

soup tāng

sour swān (*also* acid)

south nán: in the south dzài-nán-byan (located-south-side), go south shyàng-nán-byan dzǒu (towards-south-side-walk

Soviet Union Sū-lyán

space, place **dì-fang** (ground-direction)

Spain **Shĭ-băn-yá**

spare tire **bèi-tăi** (prepare-tire)

spark plugs **hwǒ-hwā-tǒu** (fire-flower-head)

speak, say **shwō**: I speak with him **wǒ gēn-ta shwō-hwà** (I with-him speak-words)

speech, to make a speech **yăn-shwō** (perform-speak)

spend money **fèi-chyán**

spike, nail **dĭng-dz**

spirit, soul **líng-hún**; spirit, ghost **gwěi**

spirit, enthusiasm **djĭng-shən** (energy-expression)

spirits **djyǒu** (*same as* wine, liquor) *or* **shāu-djyǒu** (burn-wine)

spit, to spit **tŭ-tán**

splice, knot **djyē-tǒu** (connect-head)

splint for fracture **djyă-băn** (compress-board)

splinter, chip **mù-pĭ-dz** (wood-fragment); splinter (in skin) **tsìr** (*sounds like* stab)

split, to split **pĭ**; split, cracked along the grain **pĭ-lə** (split-done)

spoil, destroy **pwò-hwài** (break-bad)

spoiled, out of order **hwài-lə** (bad-done)

sponge **hăi-myán** (sea-cotton)

spoon **sháu-dz**

sprain **nyǒu-shāng** (twist-injury)

spread something out **sàn**; spread out, deploy, disperse **sàn-kāi** (spread-open)

spring (metal) **tán-hwáng** (bounce-spring)

spring of the year **chŭn-tyan**

spy, secret agent **djyàn-dyé** (meddle-report) *or* **djyăn-shi** (traitor-mean); to spy **dāng-djyàn-dyé** *or* **dāng-djyăn-shi**

squad (of soldiers) **băn**

square **fāng-də**

squeeze **djĭ**

stab djǎ *or* tsìr

stable mǎ-hàu (horse-stable)

stack, pile dwəi: a stack of books yì-dwəi-shū (one-pile book)

staff (of assistants) tsǎn-móu

stage (in theater) wǔ-tái (act-stage)

stairs, stairway lóu-ti (building-ladder)

stake, stump djwǎng (*sounds like* to load)

stamps yóu-pyàu (mail-ticket)

standing djàn-dj (stand-remain); to stand up djàn-chi-lai (stand-up-come)

star shìng-shìng

start (machines) kǎi-kai (open-open); start, begin kǎi-shìr (open-start): start the machine bǎ-djì-chì kǎi-kai (take-machine start), start running kǎi-shír pǎu (begin run)

state, province shěng

station djàn (*also* stand): railroad station hwǒ-chə̄-djàn (fire-vehicle-station)

stationery shìn-djìr (letter-paper)

stay, live in a place djù; stay, wait děng

steady, firm wěn

steak nyóu-pái (cattle-slice)

steal tōu

steam, vapor djə̄ng-chì (evaporate-gas)

steel gǎng

steep dǒu

steering, to steer djyà-shìr

step, pace bù: a step yí-bù (one-pace)

stick, rod, shaft gǎn-dz

stick on, attach with glue djān

still hái: he's still walking tā hái-dzǒu-dj-nə (he still-walk-continue), he's still here tā hái dzài-djə̀-li (he still located-here)

stimulant shìng-fə̀n-yàu (feeling-stimulate-medicine)

stockings, socks **wǎ-dz**

stomach **wèi**

stone, rock **shír-təu** (stone-head)

stop movement **tíng-lə**; stop doing **byə́** (*same as* don't);
  stop, block, head off **lán-dju** (block-reside): the machine
  stopped **dji-chǐ tíng-lə**, he stopped the machine **tā bǎ-
  dji-chǐ tíng-lə** (he take-machine stop), stop that man
  lán-dju nà-gə rə́n, stop it **byə́ dzwə̀ nǎ-yang** (don't do
  that-manner) *or* **byə́ nǎ-yang** (don't that-manner)

stopper, plug **sāi-dz**

store **pù-dz**; bookstore **shū-pù**; clothing store **yī-dyàn**
  (clothes-shop); drugstore **yǎu-dyàn** (medicine-shop);
  grocery store **dzá-hwə-pù** (mixed-goods-store)

story, tale **gù-shir** (former-affair)

straddling **chí** (*also* to ride astride)

straight **yì-djír** (one-straight); straight line **djír-shyàn**

strap, band, tape **dǎi-dz** (*sounds like* bag)

strategy **djàn-lyuə̀** (fight-essentials)

stream, river **hə́**

street **djyə̀** (*sounds like* get, receive)

streetcar **dyàn-chə̄** (electric-vehicle)

strike, hit **dǎ**

strike, walkout **bà-gǔng** (quit-work)

string, rope **shə́ng-dz**

strong physically **chyáng-djwàng** (strong-robust); strongly
  built **djyǎn-gu** (firm-solid)

strong point **djyù-dyǎn** (holding-point)

stuck on, glued **djàn-dj** (stick-remain)

study, learn **shyuə́**; student **shyuə́-shəng** (study-person)

stuff, things **dǔng-shi**

submarine **chyán-shwə́i-tǐng** (submerge-water-barge)

substitute material **dài-yùng-pǐn** (substitute-use-article)

substitute worker **tǐ-shəu** (substitute-hand); to substitute
  for **tǐ**

subtract **djyǎn** (*also* minus)

success **chéng-gūng** (succeed-work)

suddenly **hū-rán**

suffer, hardship **shòu-kǔ** (endure-bitterness); suffer pain or sorrow **nán-gwò** (difficult-pass)

sugar, candy **táng** (*sounds like* swamp)

suggest **chū-djú-yi** (produce-suggestion)

suggestion **djú-yi**

suit **tàu** (*same as* set): a suit of clothes **yí-tàu yī-shang** (one-set clothing)

suitcase, trunk **shyāng-dz** (*also* large box)

summer **shyà-tyan** (*sounds like* down-day)

sun **tài-yang**

Sunday **lǐ-bài-tyān** (week-day)

supper, evening meal **wǎn-fàn** (late-meal); late supper **shyǎu-yè** (nocturnal-night)

supplies **gùng-yìng-pǐn** (supply-reserve-article)

support, maintain **yǎng**; support, back **yǔng-hù** (surround-protect): his father supports him **tā-də fù-chin yǎng-dj-ta** (him-belonging-father maintain-continue-him), we support our leader **wǒ-mən yǔng-hù wǒ-mən-də lǐng-shyòu** (we back us-belonging leader)

sure **yí-dìng-dwèi** (definitely-correct): I'm sure of what I say **wǒ-shwò-də yí-dìng-dwèi** (I-speak-belonging definitely-correct)

surface **myàn**: top surface **shàng-myan**

surrender **tóu-shyáng**

surround **bāu-wéi** (wrap-encircle)

suspect **hwái-yí**

swamp **táng** (*sounds like* sugar)

sweat, perspiration **hàn**; to sweat **chū-hàn** (exit-sweat)

sweater **máu-yī** (wool-clothing)

sweep **sǎu**

sweet **tyán** (*sounds like* cultivated field)

sweet potatoes **shān-yù** (mountain-tuber)

swim **yǒu-yǔng**

switch (electrical) **dyàn-mǝn** (electric-door)

switchboard **dzǔng-dji** (overall-machine)

swollen **djǔng**

sword **dà-dāu** (big-knife)

T

table **djwǝ-dz**

table, chart **byǎu** (*also* meter, watch)

tactics **djàn-shù** (fight-method)

tail **wǒi-ba** (*in the South*) *or* **yǐ-ba**

tailor **tsái-fǝng** (cut-sew)

take, hold **bǎ**

take along, lead away **dài-chyu** (lead-go)

take away (small things) **ná-chyu** (pickup-go); take away (large things) **tái-chyu** (lift-go); take apart **chāi-shyǝ** (disassemble-unload)

take care of **djàu-ying** (lookover-respond)

take off (clothes) **twǝ** (*sounds like* to tow); aircraft takes off **chǐ-fǝi** (up-fly)

take pictures **djàu-shyǎng** (shine-image)

talk, speak **shwǝ** (*also* say)

tall, high **gāu**

tame **shyùn-lyáng-dǝ** (tame-gentle-belonging)

tank (for storing liquid) **gwàn** (*same as* can); gas tank (on auto) **yǒu-shyǎng** (oil-box)

tank, armored fighting vehicle **tǎn-kǝ-chē** (tank-vehicle)

Taoism **Dàu-djyàu** (Way-teaching)

tape, band, strap **dài-dz** (*sounds like* bag); adhesive tape **djyāu-bù** (glue-cloth)

target **bǎ-dz**

tarpaulin **fán-bù** (sail-cloth)

taste, sample (food) **chǎng** (*sounds like* long); tastes good **hǎu-chǐr** (good-eat); tastes bad **bù-hǎu-chǐr** (not-good-eat)

taxes **shwèi** (*sounds like* sleep)

tea **chá**: tea leaves **chá-yè**

teach **djyǎu** (*sounds like* glue)

teacher **shyān-shəng** (first-born, *same as* Mister *and* husband)

tear up **sǐr** (*also* shredded bit, *sounds like* silk); tear apart **sǐr-kai** (tear-open)

tears (from the eyes) **yǎn-lèi** (eye-tears)

telegram **dyàn-bàu** (electric-report): to telegraph **dǎ-dyàn-bàu** (hit-telegram), telegraph set **dyàn-bàu-djī** (telegram-machine), telegraph office **dyàn-bàu-djyú** (telegram-bureau)

telephone **dyàn-hwà** (electric-words): to telephone **dǎ-dyàn-hwà** (hit-phone), phone him **dǎ-dyàn-hwà gəi-ta** (hit-phone give-him)

telescope **wàng-yuǎn-djìng** (gaze-distance-lens)

tell about, inform **gàu-sung**; tell, request, order **djyàu** (*sounds like* called): tell him about that **gàu-sung-ta nǎ-gə** (inform-him that), tell him to come **djyàu-ta lái** (order-him come)

temperature **wēn-dù** (warm-degree)

ten **shír**

tenth **dì-shír-gə** (sequence-ten-item); one tenth **shír-fən-dj yì** (ten-division-derived one)

tent **djàng-péng** (canopy-tent)

temple **myàu**

terraced fields **tī-tyán** (ladder-field)

terrain **dì-shíng** (earth-shape)

tetanus, lockjaw **pwè-shǎng-fēng** (break-injury-wind)

Thailand **Tài-gwə**; Thailander **Tài-gwə-rən** (Thai-country-person)

than **bǐ** (*same as* compare): I am bigger than he **wǒ bǐ-tā dà** (I compare-him big)

thanks **shyə̀-shyə**; many thanks **dwə̄-shyə̀**

that **nà-gə** *or* **nə̀i-gə**; that side **nà-byan**; in that way **nà-yang** (that-manner)

thatch **tsǎu** (*same as* grass)

the **nà-gə** *or* **nə̀i-gə** (*same as* that, *but usually omitted*)

theater **dyàn-yǐng-yuǎn** (movie-court) *or* **shì-yuàn-dz** (drama-court)

their, theirs **tā-mən-də** (them-belonging)

them, they **tā-mən**

then, at that time **nà-gə shír-həu** (that-time); then, in that case **djyə̀u** (*also* right away)

there **nàr** (*around Peiping*) *or* **nà-li** (that-in): he's there **tā dzài-nà-li** (he located-there), he went there **tā dàu-nà-li chyu** (he reach-there go)

therefore **swǒ-yi**

thermometer **wə̄n-dù-byǎu** (warm-degree-gage)

thermos bottle **nwǎn-shwǒi-hú** (warm-water-jar)

these **djə̀-shyə** (this-some)

they, them **tā-mən** (*used for people*) *or* **tā** (*same as* it, *used for things*): we meet them **wǒ-mən pə̀ng-djyan ta-mən**, I eat them **wǒ chīr-ta**

thick **hə̀u** (*sounds like* behind)

thief **dzə́i**

thigh **dà-twǒi** (big-leg)

thin **bǎu** *or* **shì**

thing, object **dǔng-shi**; thing, matter **shìr-ching** (matter-condition)

think, believe **shyǎng**: think it over **shyǎng-yi-shyang** (think-one-think), I think I'll come **wǒ-shyǎng wǒ lai**

(I-think I come), I believe it's so **wǒ-shyǎng shìr** (I-think be)

third one **dì-sǎn-gə** (sequence-three-item); one-third **sǎn-fēn-dj yǐ** (three-division-derived one)

thirsty **yàu-hǒ** (want-drink) *or* **kǒ**

this **djə̀-gə** *or* **djə̀i-gə**; this side **djə̀-byan**; this year **djìn-nyan**; this week **djə̀-gə lǐ-bài**; this month **djə̀-gə yuə̀**; in this way **djə̀-yang** (this-sort)

those **nà-shyə** (that-some)

thousand **chyān**; ten thousand **wàn**: a thousand **yì-chyǎn** (one-thousand), nine thousand **djyǒu-chyǎn** (nine-thousand), thirty thousand **sǎn-wàn** (three-tenthousand)

thread **shyàn** (*also* wire); screw thread **lwǒ-shyàn** (spiral-thread)

three **sǎn**

throat **sǎng-dz**

throttle, accelerator **chì-mén** (gas-door)

thru **chwǎn-gwə** (thru-cross): go thru the tunnel **chwǎn-gwə dùng chyu** (thru tunnel go)

throw **rēng**; throw away, discard **rēng-kai** (throw-open): throw that away **bǎ-nà-gə rēng-kai** (take-that throw-open)

thumb **dà-djǐr** (big-finger)

thunder **lǒi**; to thunder **dǎ-lǒi** (hit-thunder)

Thursday **lǐ-bài-sìr** (week-four)

Tibet **Shì-dzàng**: Tibetan **Shì-dzàng-də** (Tibet-belonging), Tibetan language **Shì-dzàng-hwà** (Tibet-words), Tibetan person **Shì-dzàng-rén** (Tibet person)

ticket **pyàu**

tide **cháu-shwǒi** (tide-water); high tide **gāu-cháu**; low tide **dì-cháu**

tie, cravat **lǐng-dài** (neck-band)

tie up **kún-chi-lai** (tie-up-come); tie a knot in **djì-chi-lai** (knot-up-come): tie him up **bǎ-ta kún-chi-lai** (take-him tie-up-come), he tied a knot in the rope **tā bǎ-shǒng-dz djǐ-chi-lai** (he take-rope knot-up-come)

tight closed **gwǎn-djǐn-lə**; pulled tight **lǎ-djǐn-lə**; wedged tight **shyǒ-djǐn-lə**

till, until **dǎu** (*same as* reach): till now **dǎu-shyàn-dzài** (reach-now)

time **shír-həu**: there's no time **méi-yəu shír-həu** (haven't time); one-time, once **yí-tsɨr**

tin **shí-la**

tip (money for service) **shyǎu-fǒi** (small-spend)

tire (auto) **chǒ-tǎi** (vehicle-tire)

tired out **lǎi**

to **dǎu** (*same as* reach) *or* **gǒi** (*same as* give) *or omit*: he goes to Shanghai **tā dǎu-Shǎng-hǎi chyu** (he reach-Shanghai go), sell it to him **mài gəi-ta** (sell give-him), he came to tell us **tā lǎi gǎu-sung wə-mən** (he come inform us)

tobacco, cigarettes **yǎn** (*also* smoke)

today **djǐn-tyan** (present-day)

together **yì-chǐ** (one-rise); all together, in total **yí-gùng**

toilet **tsǒ-swǒ** (latrine-structure)

tomatoes **shì-húng-shìr** (west-red-persimmon)

tomorrow **míng-tyan** (morrow-day); day after tomorrow **hǒu-tyan** (behind-day)

tonight **djǐn-tyan wǎn-shang** (today evening)

too **tài**: too big **tài-dǎ**

tools **gūng-djyù** (work-gadget)

tooth **yǎ**

top, top-side **shàng-byan**; hilltop, peak **shān-dǐng**; house top, roof **fáng-dǐng**

torn **sìr-lə** (tear-done)

total, all together **yí-gùng**

touch **mwǒ**: don't touch that thing **byǒ mwǒ nà-gə dūng-shi** tourniquet **djír-shyuǒ-dài** (stop-blood-strap)

tow, drag **twǝ**

towards, facing **shyàng** (*sounds like* resemble): towards the east **shyàng-dūng-byan**

towel **shǒu-djin** (hand-napkin)

town, city **chéng**

tracks, footprints **djyǎu-yǝr** *or* **djyǎu-yìn-dz** (foot-print); vehicle tracks, ruts **chǝ̄-dzǒu-dǝ yǝr** (vehicle-go-belonging print); railroad tracks **tyǒ-lù** (iron-road, *same as* railroad)

trace, follow up **djwǝ̄i-shyún**

tracoma **shā-yǎn** (sand-eye)

trade, commerce **mǎi-mai** (buy-sell); to trade, exchange **hwàn**

trader, merchant **mǎi-mai-rǝn** (buy-sell-person) *or* **shāng-rǝn** (commerce-person)

trailer **twǝ̄-chǝ̄** (tow-vehicle)

train **hwǒ-chǝ̄** (fire-vehicle)

training **shyùn-lyan** (teach-practise)

translate **fān-yi**

translator **fān-yi-yuán** (translate-personnel)

transmission, gear shift **byàn-sù-chì** (change-speed-device)

trap **shyǎn-djǐng** (depression-pitfall); to trap **dǎi**

travel **lyǔ-shíng**

tray **pán-dz** (*also* plate)

treat **dài** (*sounds like* to lead): he treats me very well **tā dài-wǒ hǎn-hǎu** (he treat-me very-good); to stand treat **dzwǝ̄-djǔ-rǝn** (do-host-person)

tree **shù**

trench, ditch **gǝu**

triangle **sān-djyǎu-shíng** (three-angle-shape)

trick **djì-tsǝ̄** (calculate-stratagem); to trick **shàng-dàng** (up-pawnshop): he tricked them **tā gǎi-tā-mǝn shàng-dàng** (he give-them up-pawnshop) trigger **băn-djĭ** (pry-machine)

trolley car **dyàn-chə̄** (electric-vehicle)

troops **djyŭn-dwəi** (army-team)

trouble **má-fan**

trousers **kù-dz**

truck **kă-chə̄** (car-vehicle)

true **djə̆n-də**: is it true? **shìr-bu-shir djə̆n-də** (be-not-be true)

true north **djə̀ng-bə̆i** (upright-north)

trunk, suitcase **shyăng-dz** (*also* large box)

trust, believe **shyăng-shìn**

truth **djə̆n-hwă** (true-words)

try **shìr-shir**: try to walk **dzə̆u-yi-dzəu shìr-shir** (walk-one-walk try-try)

tube, pipe **gwăn-dz**; inner tube **lĭ-tāi** (inside-tire)

Tuesday **lĭ-băi-ə̀r** (week-two)

turn, become **lə** (*tacked-on syllable*, done): it turned sour **swăn-lə** (sour-done)

turn, revolve **djwăn-dùng** (turn-move); turn over, turn around **djwăn-gwə-lai** (turn-cross-come)

turn on, switch on **kāi** (*same as* open, start); turn off **gwăn** (*same as* close)

turtle **wáng-ba** (king-eight; *to call a man turtle is an insult implying that his wife is unfaithful*)

twenty **ə̀r-shir** (two-ten)

twins **shwăng-shəng** (pair-born)

twist **nyə̆u**

two **ə̀r** *or* **lyăng** (**lyăng** is used with classifiers and measure-words, **ə̀r** is used in saying the number by itself and in building the higher numbers): two people **lyăng-gə rə̆n**, two kilometers **lyăng-gūng-lĭ**, two hundred twenty two people **ə̀r-băi-ə̀r-shir-ə̀r-gə-rə̆n**

typewrite **dă-dzìr** (hit-letters)

typewriter **dǎ-dzìr-djī** (typewrite-machine)
typhoid **shāng-hán** (injury-chill)
typhus **bān-djěn shāng-hán** (spot-measles typhoid)

U

ugly **nán-kàn** (difficult-look) *or* **bù-hǎu-kàn** (not-good-look)
umbrella **sǎn**
under **dǐ-shya** (bottom-down): it's under the table **dzài-djwō-dz dǐ-shya** (located-table under), it went under the table **dàu-djwō-dz dǐ-shya chyu** (reach-table under go)
underclothes **lǐ-yī** (inside-clothes)
understand **dǔng**: do you understand? **dǔng-bu-dung** (understand-not-understand)
uniform **djyǔn-fú** (army-dress)
union of workers **gūng-hwèi** (work-organization)
unite **lyán-hó** (join-together)
United Nations **lyán-hó-gwó**
United States of America **Měi-gwə** (*from* America, *interpreted to mean* beautiful-country)
universe **tyān-shyà** (sky-under)
university, college **dà-shyuó** (big-school)
unload cargo **shyè-hwò**, unload (gun) **twèi-dzìr-dàn** (withdraw-cartridge)
untie **djyě-kai** (solve-open)
until **dàu** (*same as* reach): until tomorrow **dàu míng-tyan**
unwrap **dǎ-bāu** (hit-wrap) *or* **dǎ-kai** (hit-open)
up **shàng** (*same as* on): the sun comes up **tài-yang shàng-lai-lə** (sun up-come), I go up the hill **wǒ shàng-shān chyu** (I up-hill go)
up, awake, arise **chǐ-lai** (riseup-come)
upstairs **lóu-shang** (building-up)
upstream **shyàng-shàng** (towards-up) *or* **shàng-shwěi** (up-water): we walked upstream **wǒ-mən shùn-dj hó shyàng-**

shǎng dzǒu (we alongside river towards-up walk), the
boat went up the river **chwán shǎng-shwǒi dzǒu-lə** (boat
up-water go-done)
upright, vertical **shù-dj-də**
urgent **djǐn-djí** (tight-haste)
urine, urinate **shyǎu-byàn** (little-convenience)
us, we **wǒ-mən**
use **yùng**
use up **yùng-wán-lə** (use-finish-done)
useful **yǒu-yùng** (have-use)
usually **pǔ-tǔng** (*also* ordinary)

V

vacationing, on vacation **fàng-djyà-lə** (put-vacation-done)
vacuum **djēn-kǔng** (true-empty)
valley **shān-gǔ** (*sounds like* mountain-drum)
valve **hwǒ-mǎn** (live-door)
vase **píng-dz** (*also* bottle)
vegetables **sù-tsài** (vegetarian-fooddish)
vehicle **chē**
vertical **shù-dj-də**
very, fairly **hěn**
veteran, experienced soldier **lǎu-bīng** (old-soldier); veteran,
discharged soldier **twài-wǔ-də bīng** (retire-rank-belong-
ing soldier)
vibrate **djàn-dùng** (shake-move)
vice-president **fù-dzúng-tǔng**
victory **shàng-lǐ**
vise **lǎu-hǔ-chyán-dz** (tiger-pliers)
village, very small town **tsūn-dz**
visit **bài-wang** *or* **kàn** (*same as* see)
volt **fú**: fifty volts **wǔ-shir-fú**
voltage **dyàn-yā** (electricity-press)

voltmeter **dyàn-yā-byǎu** (electricity-press-meter)

volume (book) **běn-dz:** three volumes **sān-běn**

volume, cubic size **tǐ-djī** (body-cumulation); volume, cubic content **rúng-lyàng** (contain-quantity)

vomit **tù**

vote **shyuán-djǔ**

W

wagon **chǝ̄** (*same as* vehicle)

wait, wait for **děng:** wait a while **děng-yi-dǝng** (wait-one-wait)

waiter **hwǒ-dji** (*also* clerk)

wake up, awake **shǐng-lǝ** (wake-done); wake someone **djyàu-shǐng** (call-wake): please wake me at seven o'clock **chǐng-nǐ chī-dyan-djung djyàu-shǐng-wǒ** (request-you seven-mark-clock call-wake-me); wake up! **shǐng-yi-shing** (wake-one-wake)

walk **dzǒu** (*also* leave): take a walk **dzǒu-yi-dzǝu** (walk-one-walk) *or* **sàn-bù** (strew-steps)

wall **chyáng**

want **yàu** (*also* will)

war **djàn-djǝ̄ng** (fight-strife)

warm, hot **rǝ̀**; the weather is pleasantly warm **tyàn-chi nwǎn-hwǝ**

warn **djǐng-gàu** (warn-inform)

wash **shǐ**

washbasin **shǐ-lyǎn-pǝ́n** (wash-face-basin)

washer, gasket **dyàn-chyuǎn** (pad-loop)

waste, to waste **làng-fǝ̀i** (extravagant-spend)

watch, clock **byǎu** (*also* chart, meter)

watch, look on at **kàn**; watch over **kǎn** (*notice different tone from* look); watchman, to guard **shǒu-wèi**; to watch, shadow, keep an eye on **lyǎu-shǝ́n** (detain-nerve) water **shwěi**

watermelon **shî-gwa** (west-melon)

watt **wǎ** (*like English*): twenty watts **ěr-shir-wǎ**

waves **làng-təu**; radio waves **dyàn-bwə̄** (electric-oscillation)

wax **là**

way, method **fá-dz**: there is no way out **méi-yəu fá-dz** (haven't way)

way, road **lù**: which way do we go? **wǒ-mən dǎ-shǒm-mə-lù dzǒu** (we hit-what-road go)

we, us **wǒ-mən**

weak **rwə̀**

weapon **bîng-chi** (soldier-device)

wear, put on (shirt, pants, socks) **chwǎn**; wear, put on (hat, tie, gloves, eyeglasses) **dài** (*sounds like* take along, lead)

weather **tyǎn-chi** (sky-gas)

weave (basketry, etc.), braid **byǎn**; weave (cloth), knit **djîr**

wedge **shyǎu-mù-pyàr** (small-wood-slice) *or* **shyə̄-dz**

Wednesday **lǐ-bài-sǎn** (week-three)

week **lǐ-bài**

weight **djùng-lyǎng** (heavy-measure); to weigh, in weight **djùng** (*also* heavy); to weigh (a thing) **chǒng-chəng**: this weighs five kilograms **djə̀-gə yǒu wǔ-gūng-djin djùng** (this have five-kilogram heavy), weigh this **bǎ-djə̀-gə chǒng-chəng** (take-this weigh)

welcome! **hwǎn-yíng**; you're welcome (in response to thanks) **bú-kə̀-chi** (not-courteous) *or* **byǒ-kə̀-chi** (don't-courteous)

weld **dǎ-hàn** (big-solder)

well for water **djǐng**

well in health **hǎu** (*same as* good)

west **shî**: in the west **dzài-shî-byan** (located-west-side), go west **shyàng-shî-byan chyu** (towards-west-side go)

wet, damp **shîr** (*sounds like* army division)

wharf **mǎ-tóu** (*sounds like* horse-head)

what? **shǎm-mə**: what's this? **djə shìr shǎm-mə** (this be what), what kind of house? **shǎm-mə-yàng-də fáng-dz** (what-manner-belonging house) *or* **shǎm-mə fáng-dz**, what do you want? **nǐ yàu shǎm-mə** (you want what), what time is it? **djí-dyǎn-djǔng-lə** (howmany-mark-clock-done)

wheat **mài-dz**; wheat foods **myàn-shir** (flour-edible)

wheel **lún-dz** *or* **gǔ-lur**

when? **shǎm-mə shír-həu** (what time); when, while **də shír-həu** (belonging time): when you came he was not home **nǐ-lái-də shír-həu tā bú-dzài-djyā** (you-come-belonging time, he not-located-home)

where? **shǎm-mə-dì-fang** (what-place) *or* **ná-li** *or* **nǎr**: where is he? **tā dzài-shǎm-mə-dì-fang** (him located-what-place), where's he going **tā dàu-shǎm-mə-dì-fang chyu** (he reach-what-place go)

which one? **nǎ-yí-gə** (which-one-item) *or* **nǎi-gə**

whistle **shàu-dz**; to whistle **chwǎi-shàu** (blow-whistle)

white **bái** (*also* pale)

who? **shǎm-mə-rən** (what-person) *or* **shwǎi**

whole **chyuán-tǐ** (whole-body)

whose? **shǎm-mə-rən-də** (what-person-belonging)

why? **wǎi-shǎm-mə** (because-what)

wide **kwān**

wife, married woman **tài-tai** (*also* Mrs.)

wild **yǒ** (*sounds like* also); wild animal **yǒ-shǎu** (wild-creature)

will **yàu** (*same as* want) *or leave it out*: he will go tomorrow **tā míng-tyan dzǒu** (he tomorrow leave)

willing **yuàn-yi** (willing-mind)

win victory **dǎ-shàng** (hit-victory); win money **yíng-chyán**

wind, breeze **fǎng**

wind around **ràu-wǎr** *or* **ràu-wǎn-dz** (wind-bend)

window **chwăng-hu**

wine, liquor **dyjŏu** (*sounds like* nine *and* long time)

wing **chĭr-băng**

winter **dŭng-tyan**

wipe **tsă**

wire, cable **shyàn** (*also* thread); barbed wire **yŏu-tsĭr tyŏ-sĭr** (have-thorn iron-strand)

wise **tsŭng-ming** (wise-bright)

wish **yàu-shir dwə̄-hău** (if, how-good): I wish I could **wŏ yàu-shir nə́ng dwə̄-hău** (I if able, how-good); wish, pray **djú**: I wish you a safe journey **djú-nĭ yí-lù píng-ăn** (pray-you one-road safe)

with, along with **gə̄n** (*also* follow); with, by **yùng** (*same as* use) *or* **dzwə̀** (*same as* sit): I come with him **wŏ gə̄n-ta lái** (I with-him come), I do it with a knife **wŏ yùng-dău-dz dzwə̀** (I use-knife do), I come with the train **wŏ dzwə̀-hwŏ-chə̄ lái** (I sit-train come)

without **bù-gə̄n** (not-with) *or* **bú-yùng** (not-use): I come without him **wŏ bù-gə̄n-ta lái** (I not-with-him come), I cooked without salt **wŏ bú-yùng-yán dzwə̀-fàn** (I not-use-salt make-food)

woman **nyŭ-rən**

wood **mù-təu** (wood-head)

woods **shù-lín-dz** (tree-forest)

wool **mău-rúng** (hair-fuzz)

wool cloth **ní** (*sounds like* mud)

words, speaking **hwà**; written words, characters, letters **dzĭr**

work, labor **gŭng-dzwə̀** (work-do); work, business, matter **shĭr** (*sounds like* be); to work **dzwə̀-gŭng** (do-work) *or* **dzwə̀-shĭr** (do-job)

worker **gŭng-rən** (work-person)

workshop **dji-chĭ-fáng** (machine-device-house)

world **shìr-djyə**

worm **chúng-dz**

worn out, broken down **hwài-lə** (*also* spoiled); worn out, tired **lèi**

worry **fā-chóu** (issue-melancholy)

worship, attend services **dzwò lǐ-bài** (do worship)

worship, admire **chúng-bài**

worse **hwài-yi-dyar** (bad-one-bit)

worst **dzwèi-hwài** (most-bad)

wound, injury **shāng**; wounded **fù-shāng** (bear-injury)

wrap up **bāu-chi-lai** (wrap-up-come)

wrench **bǎn-shǒu** (pry-hand)

write **shyǒ**: I can write **wǒ hwèi-shyǒ-dzìr** (I knowhow-write-characters), write a letter **shyǒ-shìn**

wrong **tswò-də** (mistake-belonging) *or* **tswò-lə** (mistake-done)

YZ

yams (one variety) **shān-yàu** (mountain-medicine); yams, sweet potatoes **shān-yù** (mountain-tuber)

yard, court **yuàn-dz**

yard of length **mǎ** (*sounds like* horse), *but the official measure is the meter* **gūng-chǐr** (universal-lengthmeasure)

year **nyán**: one-year **yì-nyán**, this year **djìn-nyan** (present-year), last year **chyù-nyan** (go-year), next year **míng-nyan** (morrow-year)

year old **swèi**: a year old **yí-swèi** (one-ageyear)

yellow **hwáng**

yes: *use expressions like* it's so **shìr** *or* it's O.K. **hǎu**

yesterday **dzwó-tyan** (yester-day); day before yesterday **chyán-tyan** (previous-day)

yet **hái** (*same as* still): has he come yet? **tā hái lái-bu-lai** (he still come-not-come)

yoke (for hitching) *or* carrying-pole (carried by one man)
dàn-dz

you (one person) **nǐ**; you people **nǐ-mən**

young, youthful **nyán-ching** (year-light) *or* **shàu**; young,
not grown up **shyǎu** (*same as* small)

your, yours **nǐ-də** (you-belonging) *or* **nǐ-mən-də** (youpeople-
belonging)

zero **líng**